Praise for *We Can't Talk about That at Work!*

"I'm very excited about the release of *We Can't Talk about That at Work!* The issue of discussing polarizing topics at work is a really tough one. People are not comfortable having uncomfortable conversations. I'm happy that there will finally be a resource to guide us all on how to get comfortable being uncomfortable."
  —Michele C. Meyer-Shipp, Esq., Vice President and Chief Diversity Officer, Prudential Financial, Inc.

"This book is a comprehensive, practical, and highly accessible tool for empowering people to have the brave conversations that are needed in these tumultuous times. Mary-Frances has given readers an invaluable resource for organizations and individuals to navigate the charged times that we live in and make a contribution toward cocreating a more compassionate future."
  —Nene Molefi, diversity and inclusion thought leader and CEO, Mandate Molefi, Johannesburg, South Africa

"Mary-Frances Winters's wisdom shines throughout this book. She helps us understand deeply why we need to talk about polarizing topics—yes, at work—and then proceeds to show us how with care, concern, and compassion for those who may not agree with us. I hope that all leaders and employees read it and implement her wise suggestions and counsel."
  —Julie O'Mara, coauthor of *Global Diversity and Inclusion Benchmarks* and other inclusion works and Past-President, American Society for Training & Development (now ATD)

"We are living in times of crisis. Day after day, we are confronted with polarization about issues of real import to our society and our world that can seem difficult, if not impossible, to talk about. And yet this is not a time for timidity. We must talk about these issues if we are going to cross the great divides in our ideologies and exist together in civil society. Mary-Frances Winters has created an extremely helpful guide for better understanding and navigating those difficult conversations. Be bold—use this book!"
  —Howard Ross, founder and Chief Learning Officer, Cook Ross

P9-CJK-175

"*We Can't Talk about That at Work!* has hit the mark. This body of work is critically important to advancing inclusion and dialogue in our workplaces. As we work diligently to increase our diversity, we struggle with inclusion and having the difficult conversations about the various aspects of diversity. Now, we have a road map and tools to support diversity professionals, leaders, and employees in any work environment. This will be the book used by all."
—**Darlene Slaughter, Vice President and Chief Diversity Officer, United Way Worldwide**

"In the current global political and social climate, characterized by increasingly polarized views, the ability to embrace views different from our own, without judgment or vilification, is more critical than ever. It is also at the heart of all diversity and inclusion work. For with all our ideals, we often overlook the fact that diversity and inclusion can be hard. In *We Can't Talk about That at Work!*, Mary-Frances addresses this issue head-on, providing practical skills to empower leaders and managers to have effective dialogue across difference."
—**Kate Vernon, Director, Strategic Programmes, Asia, Community Business**

"The presidential farewell address is a perfect way to set up this powerful and practical guide to effectively engaging in conversations about polarizing issues. I too believe that we need to meet people where they are, and not expect them to necessarily see the world from our view, and that we *all* have work to do to close the cultural divide and change hearts. What makes this book different is its soft approach to bold conversations, using talking tips, templates, and reflection questions."
—**Tyronne Stoudemire, Vice President of Global Diversity and Inclusion, Hyatt Hotels Corporation, and Adjunct Lecturer of Management and Organization, Kellogg School of Management, Northwestern University**

"Whether in her writing, public speaking, or consulting, Mary-Frances Winters always delivers. Deep subject matter expertise, strategic thinking, sociocultural insights, contemporary application, and wisdom will spill out of these pages as you engage with them."
—**Andrés Tapia, Senior Client Partner and Global Practice Leader, Workforce Performance, Inclusion and Diversity, Korn Ferry Hay Group, and author of *The Inclusion Paradox***

WE CAN'T TALK ABOUT THAT AT WØRK!

WE CAN'T TALK ABOUT THAT AT WØRK!

HOW TO TALK ABOUT
RACE, RELIGION, POLITICS, AND OTHER POLARIZING TOPICS

MARY-FRANCES WINTERS

BK·

Berrett–Koehler Publishers, Inc.
a BK Business book

Berrett-Koehler Publishers, Inc.
1333 Broadway, Suite 1000
Oakland, CA 94612-1921
Tel: (510) 817-2277
Fax: (510) 817-2278
www.bkconnection.com

ORDERING INFORMATION

Quantity sales. Special discounts are available on quantity purchases by corporations, associations, and others. For details, contact the "Special Sales Department" at the Berrett-Koehler address above.

Individual sales. Berrett-Koehler publications are available through most bookstores. They can also be ordered directly from Berrett-Koehler: Tel: (800) 929-2929; Fax: (802) 864-7626; www.bkconnection.com.

Orders for college textbook/course adoption use. Please contact Berrett-Koehler: Tel: (800) 929-2929; Fax: (802) 864-7626.

Distributed to the U.S. trade and internationally by Penguin Random House Publisher Services.

Berrett-Koehler and the BK logo are registered trademarks of Berrett-Koehler Publishers, Inc.

Printed in the United States of America

Berrett-Koehler books are printed on long-lasting acid-free paper. When it is available, we choose paper that has been manufactured by environmentally responsible processes. These may include using trees grown in sustainable forests, incorporating recycled paper, minimizing chlorine in bleaching, or recycling the energy produced at the paper mill.

Library of Congress Cataloging-in-Publication Data
Names: Winters, Mary-Frances, author.
Title: We can't talk about that at work! : how to talk about race, religion, politics, and other polarizing topics / Mary-Frances Winters.
Description: First edition. | Oakland : Berrett-Koehler Publishers, [2017] | Includes bibliographical references and index.
Identifiers: LCCN 2017005637 | ISBN 9781523094264 (pbk. : alk. paper)
Subjects: LCSH: Communication in organizations. | Interpersonal communication. | Interpersonal relations. | Organizational sociology.
Classification: LCC HD30.2 .W5636 2017 | DDC 650.1/3--dc23
LC record available at https://lccn.loc.gov/2017005637

First Edition

22 21 20 19 18 | 10 9 8 7 6 5 4 3

Produced and designed by BookMatters, copyedited by Tanya Grove, proofed by Janet Reed Blake, indexed by Leonard Rosenbaum. Cover design by Irene Morris / Morris Design

*To the generations of freedom fighters, civil rights
leaders, and social justice advocates who preceded
me in the ongoing quest for an inclusive, equitable
world that values the dignity of all people.*

*And especially to those who lost their lives in the struggle.
Without their sacrifice, my voice would not be possible.*

For too many of us it's become safer to retreat into our own bubbles, whether in our neighborhoods, or on college campuses, or places of worship, or especially our social media feeds, surrounded by people who look like us and share the same political outlook and never challenge our assumptions. . . . All of us have more work to do. . . . Hearts must change. . . . But without some common baseline of facts, without a willingness to admit new information and concede that your opponent might be making a fair point . . . then we're going to keep talking past each other. . . . None of this is easy.

BARACK H. OBAMA
44TH PRESIDENT
UNITED STATES OF AMERICA
FAREWELL ADDRESS
JANUARY 10, 2017

Contents

Preface

Don't talk about race, politics, or religion at work!

Whether we like it or not, or are prepared for it or not, this adage no longer applies. People are talking about these issues, or at minimum, thinking about them, and it impacts productivity, engagement, and employees' sense of safety and well-being. Considering we have been taught not to talk about polarizing topics, especially at work, we may not know how to do it very well. Thus, our attempts may lead to counterproductive, divisive dialogue. And as our workplaces become more diverse, these conversations are ever more complicated.

Effectively engaging in bold, inclusive conversations is hard work and is getting even harder due to the current global, political, and social climate. Many great leaders have attempted with some success over the years to bring people across varying dimensions of difference to the table to alleviate the **polarization**, animosity, and hatred that has plagued the human race since the beginning of time.

I contend that the reason we are not further along—and perhaps regressing—is because we have not approached the

Words in the text that are **sans serif bold** are defined in the glossary.

work in a developmental way. We have failed to fully realize and understand that not everybody is ready for bold conversations. If we were to approach the work developmentally, we would meet people where they are, not expect them to necessarily see the world from our view, and acknowledge that while one may be learning, mistakes are inevitable.

Someone who is just learning to ride a bike will fall off. If you ask someone to solve an advanced algebra problem before taking Algebra 101, he/she will likely be unsuccessful and may give up. I urge us to cut each other some slack—be patient, encouraging, and forgiving. In Malcolm Gladwell's book, *The Outliers*, he asserts that it takes 10,000 hours of practice to achieve mastery in any skill. And I posit that once you have achieved mastery, let's say as an accomplished pianist, you still don't stop practicing. You never stop learning new pieces. The same is true for engaging in bold, inclusive conversations.

We Can't Talk about That at Work! provides an effective guide to developing the skills necessary to engage in conversations around polarizing topics, acknowledging that these topics are complex, that there are no simple answers, and that it takes time and practice to learn how to do it well. Keep in mind that this book is a guide and not a prescription for how to have bold, inclusive conversations. There is no one right answer and no one fail-proof model. Throughout the book, I try to give you a myriad of things to consider before embarking on a difficult conversation, as well as some examples of what may work and why other approaches may not.

Over the past 20 years, we have witnessed increased and intensified global polarization on many topics related to our differences. Unfortunate acts of terrorism, incidents that spurred movements like Black Lives Matter, Brexit (fueled by xenophobia), and the divisiveness of the 2016 US presidential election are leaving indelible wounds on many. We see vast divisions that exacerbate an "us-and-them" disunity, leading to heightened racism, xenophobia, Islamophobia, classism, and homophobia.

We are failing to find a shared purpose that binds all of humanity together. Rather than moving more toward shared meaning and understanding, as President Barack Obama said in his farewell address, we are staying in our own corners with like-minded people, entrenched in our own ideologies, unable to find a common vision.

I wrote *We Can't Talk about That at Work!* in response to clients of The Winters Group wanting tools and resources that would support them in engaging employees in effective and authentic conversations around these unfortunate events. We found there was a growing desire among leaders and employees to have these conversations but a lack of competence to do so effectively.

This practical guide will support you in answering some of the following questions:

- As an individual who has been personally impacted by some of the unfortunate events of our time, how do you maintain your level of engagement at work? How do you share your feelings and thoughts with your manager or coworkers? Is there a level of trust present to engage in topics like race, religion, and politics?

- You may not personally feel that you are impacted by some of these events but empathize with coworkers who have been. How can you become an effective, supportive ally and build trust among diverse coworkers? What skills are required to initiate these conversations?

- As a leader, how do you manage diverse employees who have different perspectives and experiences? How do you encourage and facilitate inclusive conversations about polarizing topics so that all employees feel valued, respected, and safe?

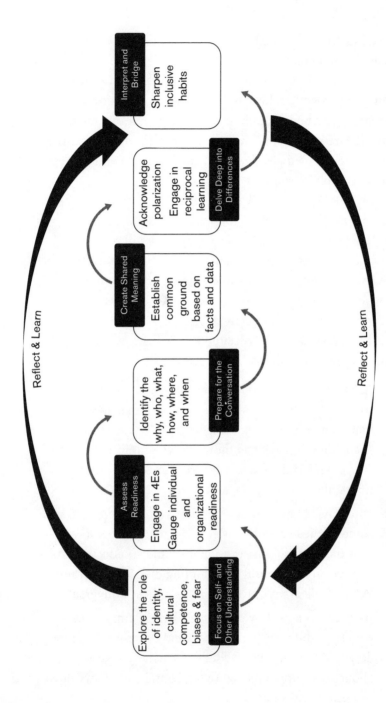

FIGURE 1. A MODEL FOR BOLD, INCLUSIVE CONVERSATIONS

We Can't Talk about That at Work! lays out a blueprint for developing the skills necessary to effectively engage in conversations about polarizing issues. Figure 1 (A Model for Bold, Inclusive Conversations) depicts a process for engaging in these conversations and will serve as the structural sequence for the book. In Chapter 1, we explore the business case for engaging in bold conversations in the workplace. The subsequent chapters expound on each phase presented in this figure.

If you are interested in engaging in conversations to create a more inclusive world, this book will start you on your journey.

Thank you for your interest in my book.

Yours inclusively,

Mary-Frances Winters

ONE

◆ ◆ ◆

Why Do We Have to Talk about **THAT** at Work?

High performing leaders are able to unite
diverse team members by building common
goals and even shared emotions by engaging
in powerful and effective dialogue.

GEORGE KOHLRIESER,
Clinical and Organizational Psychologist[1]

Why in the world would we want to encourage employees to talk about polarizing topics in the workplace? We come to work in order to make products and provide services for our customers, members, and/or clients—not to talk about social issues. Topics such as race, politics, and religion are inappropriate and should be discouraged.

Perhaps this is how you feel. For as long as I can remember, this has been the prevailing sentiment for many organizations and corporate environments. However, there are compelling reasons why a position of avoidance is no longer the best policy.

The most persuasive reason for building the skills necessary to talk about polarizing topics at work is that they are already being talked about or thought about, more than you may think. Social media is a huge factor in the increased visibility of and exposure to these issues. And even as these topics remain top of mind for most of us, in general, we lack the skills to have effective dialogue.

The goal of this book is to help you make the conversations that are already happening more productive, supportive, and inclusive, leaving people feeling whole and ultimately resulting in better teamwork, productivity, and engagement.

A POLARIZED SOCIETY LEADS TO
A POLARIZED WORKPLACE

When race enters our public conversations about these important national issues, the dialogue is too often dehumanizing and racially charged. Language matters, and we need more tools to move our race conversations forward in more accurate, fair, and productive ways.

President Barack Obama [2]

As the workforce becomes more diverse, there are more people from different racial/ethnic groups, religious affiliations, political affiliations, sexual orientations, and **disability** statuses who may be facing very different realities than ever before. We are living in times of heightened social conflict around race, religion, and politics. The last few years have been filled with instances of police brutality, the shooting and killing of police officers, immigration debates, religious intolerance against Muslims and Jews, heightened awareness of transgender rights and its backlash, terrorism, and extreme political divisions, making it impossible for many *not* to bring strong emotions about these issues into the workplace.

Social scientists contend that the more we feel threatened, the greater our tendency to be "tribal" and polarized. Tribalism is part of human nature. We've found that many people feel that their way of life is being threatened by terrorism, demographic changes, and new technology. When people are fearful, the gut level response is to blame "the other tribe(s)" for their plight. With so many complex issues facing society today, there is more polarization than ever before. Consider these realities:

- In a 2016 survey that explored the state of race relations in the United States, only 44 percent of white people were very concerned about the killings of black people at the hands of police, compared to 77 percent of black responders. However, when asked about the killings of police officers in Dallas, over 75 percent of *both* black and white people were very concerned.[3]

- In a survey on race and workplace trauma conducted by The Winters Group, six in ten whites answered that they think their organization understands the unique experiences of blacks in the workplace. In direct contrast six in ten blacks answered that they did *not* think their organization understands their unique experiences.[4]

- The vote for Britain to exit the European Union has largely been attributed to class issues and xenophobia. A headline in the *Guardian* in June 2016 read, "BREXIT is the only way the working class can change anything."[5] The results of the election showed deep class divides. Many working-class Brits blame immigration for the loss in jobs. Between 1993 and 2014, the number of immigrants into the UK surged from 3.8 million to 8.3 million.[6]

- A recent poll showed that 56 percent of Americans feel that Muslim values are at odds with US values. However, 68 percent said that they had never or seldom talked to a Muslim.[7]

- In a Pew survey on gender equality, 56 percent of men said that obstacles inhibiting women's progress are largely gone. Only 34 percent of women shared that view.[8]

- According to a global study conducted by Unilever based on interviews with 9,000 men and women across eight global markets, stereotypes and inappropriate behavior targeting women in the workplace still prevail. Sixty-seven percent of women in the study reported that they feel pressured to "get over" inappropriate behavior, and 55 percent of men and 64 percent of women believe that men do not challenge each other when they witness such behavior.[9]

- Relative to political polarization in the United States, a Pew study showed that 93 percent of Republicans are more conservative than the median Democrat, while a nearly identical share of Democrats (94 percent) is more liberal than the median Republican. Twenty years ago, there was a much smaller divide, with 64 percent of Republicans to the right of the median Democrat, and 70 percent of Democrats to the left of the median Republican.[10]

- The inauguration of Donald Trump as the 45th president of the United States drew strong protests around the world. Globally, over three million people participated in the Women's March to protest the election of President Trump, who they feel does not represent the values espoused by the United States, especially those policies geared toward gender equality, health care for women, religious freedom, and **LGBTQ** rights. Protesters said that they joined the marches because of Trump's divisive campaign and his disparagement of women, minorities, and immigrants.[11]

- The North Carolina HB2 bill, known as the "bathroom bill," requires transgender people to use public bathrooms associated with their birth sex.[12] As a result, a number of organizations cancelled high-profile events in the state, resulting in millions of dollars of lost revenue.

◆ Environmental justice and racism, both highly political subjects, intersected in mid-2016 when the US Army Corps of Engineers authorized the Dakota Access Pipeline project (DAPL), which threatened the safety and sanctity of the Standing Rock Sioux tribe's water and sacred cultural sites. The project sparked national protests and a grassroots movement that sought to reaffirm the humanity of indigenous people and their land. The DAPL has sparked polarization among business, political, and Native American communities.[13]

◆ There has been ongoing dissention around the term "Redskin" and other mascots that denigrate Native American communities. As of 2010, over 115 professional organizations—representing civil rights advocates, educational institutions, athletes, and scientific experts—have published resolutions or policies that state that the use of Native American names and/or symbols by non-native sports teams is a harmful form of ethnic stereotyping that promotes misunderstanding and prejudice, which contributes to other problems faced by Native Americans.[14] However, as of the publication date of this book, the Washington, DC, football team has not changed its name.

◆ We see a great deal of polarization and discourse around immigration. A range of countermeasures have been put forth—from building a wall to the more liberal proposal of the Dream Act, a multi-phased process for undocumented residents to provide conditional residency leading to permanent status. Due in part to political dissention, the bill never passed.[15]

◆ While conversations about disability and people with disabilities may not be deemed as polarizing, I have found that we shy away from the subject matter, even in discussions around diversity. Perhaps this is because we do not know how to effectively have these bold conversations. In 2014, the British charity Scope conducted a survey that found two-thirds of British people feel uncomfortable or awkward talking to somebody who is disabled.[16]

Kate Vernon, director of strategy programs at Community Business and author of extensive research on diversity and inclusion in Asia, makes this observation:

> It can be difficult to have open and honest conversations about race in Asia. We often talk about **culture** and the impact of different cultural profiles on communication and working styles—but we rarely address the biases and prejudices that exist about or between different ethnic groups, or openly acknowledge the power and **privilege** that certain groups enjoy. But there is no doubt that racism does exist in Asia. Whether it be India or Hong Kong, Japan or Singapore, there is an unspoken, often complex racial hierarchy that many will recognize but be wary to articulate. If we are to promote a culture of true inclusion, we need to find a way to broach this sensitive topic. Yet the Asian preference for promoting harmony, saving face, and showing respect can make having such bold conversations doubly hard.[17]

These polarized views and often-avoided topics drive attitudes, perceptions, and behaviors. If I no longer believe there are barriers for women in the workplace, I would see no need for special programs designed to bolster women's chances for advancement. If I am not concerned about the shootings of unarmed black men, then I may not be empathetic to workers who are fearful and traumatized by such events.

POLARIZATION THWARTS INCLUSION; INCLUSION DRIVES ENGAGEMENT

Polarization thwarts attempts for inclusion. Polarization is the opposite of inclusion. Polarization fosters an "us-and-them" environment, whereas inclusion attempts to create a sense of belonging and unity. Most major organizations today have a goal to create an inclusive culture because they realize that inclusion drives engagement. As reported in a 2013 Gallup study, inclusion and engagement are highly correlated.[18] The results showed that the most engaged employees rated the company high on diversity and inclusion. The least engaged employees rated the company very low on the questions related to diversity and inclusion. The Winters Group conducted a survey with a large financial institution that showed similar results. Inclusion was the highest correlated factor to engagement.

When employees feel that they are psychologically safe, they are also more engaged and innovative. According to a study by Catalyst that surveyed Australian workers, employees who experience psychological safety feel that they can freely speak up about problems and tough issues.[19] One's perception of psychological safety is based on a belief about the organization's norms or culture, which I cover in Chapter 3. The same study identified four leadership characteristics that enable psychological safety across race, gender, and other demographic variables. They are accountability, courage, humility, and empowerment. I speak to courage and **cultural humility** in Chapter 2.

THE IMPACT OF SOCIAL MEDIA ON POLARIZATION

Social media outlets are exacerbating the increase in polarization. Instantaneous access to breaking news and opinions via tools such as Twitter, Facebook, Snapchat, and others has magnified opportunities to engage in contentious conversation and debate. People routinely use their smart phones to record all sorts of events that go viral for the whole world to see and comment on.

Before social media, we weren't as likely to be constantly confronted with polarizing topics such as race, religion, and politics unless we were news junkies. In the workplace, it is easy, even if against company policy, to have ongoing access to social media on our smart devices. Therefore, many people are constantly debating and sharing their opinions and beliefs on social media; and to the extent that they are virtually connected to coworkers, they are having these conversations at work, or in a workplace context. Social media makes it very easy to know the beliefs and opinions of coworkers.

The more that an individual's personal beliefs are repeated (i.e., go viral), the more they become accepted as fact. By the same token, the more an individual's or a group's beliefs are challenged, the more they are believed by that group. When beliefs are challenged, the human tendency is to become more obstinate and determined to defend the opinion. In other words, we dig our heels in deeper, as the saying goes. Any attention to the belief or opinion, positive or negative, acts as fuel for the fire.

Let's take Facebook, for example. The personal nature of this form of electronic communication can keep our emotions in high gear. We tell our Facebook friends what we like and what we don't like. When we disagree with a friend on Facebook we continue to post more rationale for our own position, and they, in turn, post more for their position, increasing the polarization. In the extreme, when a friend posts something we don't like, we can "un-friend" them. In other words, we can stay firmly rooted in our own beliefs, totally rejecting another's viewpoint. We take an "I don't want to hear it" attitude and in some cases, an "I don't like you anymore." We are often unable to separate the person from their position. I discuss the need to separate the person from the position in Chapter 3.

Many people today are addicted to social media. Social and behavioral scientists are busy studying the psychological ramifications of this fairly new phenomenon. I have talked with many people who say they have disconnected from social media and now feel less stressed. Some, who have not done so, bring these intense emotions and associated anxiety with them to work. And they do not stop communicating on polarizing issues just because they are at work.

THE IMPACT ON EMPLOYEES, IN THEIR OWN WORDS

The Winters Group has conducted a number of dialogue sessions for a variety of different clients over the past year, supporting them in effectively addressing the aftermath of recent traumatic events and the polarized views that seem to always be associated with them. My first request is "Describe how you are feeling in one word." The responses range from depressed, despondent, frustrated, angry, helpless, and hopeless to encouraged, energized, hopeful, and optimistic. However, a majority of the emotions are negative.

Psychologists believe that the recurrence of unfortunate events intensifies feelings of stress and trauma. The more we see images of police shootings, terrorist attacks, and other acts of violence, the more we are likely to experience effects likened to post traumatic stress syndrome. Individuals who are most impacted by these events—for instance, black men fearful that they will be wrongly targeted by police, Muslim women in hijabs afraid they will be subject to bullying or worse, transgendered employees afraid to use the bathroom that corresponds to their gender identities—are likely distracted at work. This impacts engagement and productivity.

The Winters Group has conducted several public, free virtual learning webinars to address some of these issues. One was called Race & Workplace Trauma during the Age of #BlackLivesMatter. More than 250 people were in attendance. Another, called Let the Healing Begin: Restoring Our Quest for Inclusion, was conducted immediately following the 2016 presidential election. Over 600 registered for this 90-minute session. We polled participants during both sessions to explore the extent to which these events impacted their productivity at work. More than 60 percent admitted that there was either a "great deal" or "somewhat" of an impact.

Here are some perspectives shared during these sessions:

"I came to work the day after the Philando Castile killing and I said to my boss that I was pretty upset, and I got nothing, not even an acknowledgment. This really shook me up and now I don't know if I can really trust her."[20]
—*African American male at large consulting company*
   (I heard similar sentiments from several others from different companies.)

"I am Muslim, gay, and from the Middle East. That is three strikes against me. When I am waiting for the train at the metro station I don't stand near the edge because I am afraid someone might push me in. I bring that fear to work with me every day. It does impact my ability to concentrate and do my best work."
—*male employee at a not-for-profit research organization*

"I was at work and got a call from my child at school. He was terrified because the kids were telling him that he

was going to be deported. I felt a need to leave and go and get him. My boss understood."
—*Latina employee at a large service organization*

"Our company sent out a statement after the Pulse Night Club shooting[21] but said nothing about the killings of unarmed black men. Why does one group deserve acknowledgment and sympathy and our group [African Americans] does not?"
—*African American employee at a large consulting firm*
    (I heard similar statements from African Americans at
    several different companies.)

"I have not been affected by these events at all. I could not have imagined the impact that it is having on you. It is shocking to me that you are fearful based on who you are."
—*white senior leader in a not-for-profit research organization*

"I work from home. I am isolated. I don't know what the sentiment is at the company really. I just know that my ability to stay focused on work has been impacted. I did look for a message from leadership. I think it would have helped."
—*African American woman at a large consulting firm*

"One of my coworkers was literally gloating after Donald Trump won the presidential election. I don't mind showing happiness that your candidate won, but the tone was like, 'See, now you people will have to know your place again.'"
—*African American woman at a government agency*

"As a Muslim doctor, I have patients who ask for a different physician because they do not want to be seen by a Muslim. I have colleagues who are visiting nurses, who

have doors shut in their faces when they arrive for home health care services because of the color of their skin. We have to talk about these issues in the workplace."
—*Muslim doctor at a large health-care organization*

"I am the only person of Middle Eastern descent on my team. I overhear conversations about terrorists, but they never discuss that with me. As a matter of fact, I think they purposefully avoid such conversations around me. It makes me feel isolated. I don't really feel like I am a part of the team."
—*Muslim engineer at a large technology company*

While over the past five years, our awareness of traumatizing events has increased, unreported incidences of unequal treatment that impact **historically marginalized groups** are certainly not new.

Fifteen years ago, I was conducting a diversity strategy session for a large insurance company in the Midwest. It was a three-day event comprised of senior leaders who were charged with developing the company's inclusion strategy. On the second day, one of the African American male participants arrived a few minutes late. He was visibly distracted. Later, I learned that he had been stopped by the police on his way to the session, which was held at a venue in a high-income part of town. No infraction had occurred. The police officer asked to see his license and wanted to know where he was going. He was asked where he lived, where he worked, and what brought him to that area.

This incident was extremely disturbing to this African American executive. He did not want to share the incident publicly with the rest of the group, even though it was a diversity session, because his organization, in his estimation, was not ready to really deal with such issues. He admitted to me that it was difficult for him to continue to engage in the session.

How many people are bringing similar stresses with them to work as a result of being targeted just because of what they look like? How many feel that they must suffer in silence?

COMPANY SILENCE TRANSLATES INTO "YOU DON'T CARE"

During The Winters Group's virtual learning sessions, we asked: "What is the impact when your manager and your company are silent about what is going on in the external world?" The most common response is "We don't think they care." Employees who are impacted, either directly or indirectly, by these events are looking for their companies to say something. Organizations do not operate in a bubble; what is happening in the external world has a direct impact on employees, and they are talking about it at work whether we like it or not.

CEO's Story Reveals Aha Moment

AT&T's CEO, Randall Stephenson, made a public statement at an employee meeting about Black Lives Matter. "Our communities are being destroyed by racial tension and we're too polite to talk about it," referring to shootings and protests in Charlotte, North Carolina; Ferguson, Missouri; Baton Rouge, Louisiana; and Dallas, Texas.[22]

Stephenson also shared a story of his struggles with understanding the US racial divide. One of Stephenson's longtime friends who happens to be African American, provided an aha experience for him. Stephenson said that he learned that his friend's life as an African American male doctor is fraught with being called negative names, being mistaken for the server in restaurants, and needing to always carry his ID, even in his own neighborhood, because of experiences with law enforcement.

Stephenson told his employees that he was embarrassed that he had known this man for many years, had shared intimate moments, counted him as one of his best friends, and had no idea of his daily struggles as a black man in America. At the end of his speech, the employees cheered. In that moment, Stephenson made himself vulnerable and passionately articulated the compelling reason for having the courage to dialogue about our differences. The world now knows Stephenson's stance. The video has garnered over 160,000 YouTube views. In an increasingly competitive hiring market, I think this will boost efforts to attract diverse talent to AT&T.

Company's Proactive Approach Leads the Way

Sodexo is a company that is routinely heralded for its progressive inclusive practices. It has been number one on *DiversityInc*'s list of top 50 companies for diversity several times and has won a number of other awards for diversity and inclusion. It is also taking a proactive approach in supporting employees in navigating the current social and political environment. The company has issued several statements letting employees know that it cares and advising them on where they can seek support internally.

In addition, The Winters Group has designed several virtual learning labs for Sodexo's inclusion community, including HR and employee network group leaders, to provide tools and tips for engaging in bold conversations. The 90-minute learning sessions, entitled Affirming Inclusion: Meaningful Dialogue across Difference, explore strategies for maintaining inclusive environments after tragedies.

After the 2016 election, The Winters Group hosted a

learning lab for Sodexo employees entitled Moving Forward: Reaffirming Our Commitment to Inclusion, with the goal of examining feelings after the results of the divisive 2016 presidential election and reaffirming what it means to be inclusive. The content was balanced, recognizing that their employees represent all political parties. We explored the complex reasons for political polarization, including the socio-economic divide, lingering effects of the 2008 recession, influence of social media, worsening race relations, and technological advances that are replacing human workers with automated solutions.

In addition to the virtual learning labs, Sodexo has a page on its diversity and inclusion site called Inclusion Amidst Turbulent Times—Fostering Understanding across Differences. It acknowledges the pain associated with the violence and terrorism and provides employees with several internal resources for different groups, including blacks/African Americans, immigrant employees, Muslims, and the LGBTQ community.

Sodexo's website is proactive in providing employees with tools to dialogue across difference. It believes that offering these resources will improve employees' overall sense of well-being and thus improve engagement. It is consistent with Sodexo's mission of "improving the quality of life for those they serve."

Virtual Learning Labs Provide Tools

A large trade association attended one of The Winters Group's public virtual sessions on race-based trauma. Following that, the organization hosted a series of what it calls Health Hints to continue to discuss the topic and provide employees with coping strategies and tips on how to be an ally. In conjunction with these efforts, they retained The Winters Group to offer a virtual learning opportunity to further enhance employees' capabilities in having culturally competent, constructive conversations around race and trauma. The session explored the current state of race relations and implications for the workplace and provided strategies for engaging in meaningful dialogue around race. The evaluations showed that employees who attended felt better equipped to manage the stressors and to engage in effective dialogue.

ENGAGING IN CONVERSATIONS SENDS THE SIGNAL THAT AN ORGANIZATION CARES

There has been a consensus among participants that just allowing the opportunity for the dialogue is cathartic and sends a message that the organization is sensitive to the impact of these types of events. Most say that they just wanted to be able to share their feelings and hear how others may be coping. However, progressive companies recognize that this initial sharing session is not enough. People may feel better for the moment, but despite heightened awareness, there are no solutions. In order for effective dialogue to continue, employees need the skills necessary to go deeper in fostering mutual understanding. Skill building takes time, which is why Sodexo conducts ongoing skill-building training for its employees. Chapters 5 and 6 focus on building and practicing the skills.

You may not be able to precisely account for the loss of productivity caused by the emotional toll of tragic events or immediately gauge the enhanced engagement that may come from employers' acknowledging the impact, but it can be significant. Taking a proactive approach demonstrates to employees that the company cares and wants to be supportive. It is critical to develop ways to have meaningful conversations across difference. In the end, it will help to create an environment that allows every employee to feel like they belong.

CHAPTER 1 ◆ TIPS FOR TALKING ABOUT IT!

◆ Recognize that whether we think it is right or not, employees are talking about topics like race, religion, politics, and other polarizing topics in the workplace.

◆ Because workplaces are increasingly diverse with different racial/ethnic groups, religions, sexual orientations, and so on, you will need to pay attention to the needs of different groups if you want to engage all employees.

◆ Realize that the tragic events that are occurring in our world impact different groups in different ways and can negatively influence productivity, engagement, and employees' sense of safety.

◆ Recognize that employees bring their fears and other emotions into the workplace.

◆ Promote inclusion and provide resources to support employees in addressing their concerns.

◆ Provide tools and resources to develop skills to effectively talk about polarizing topics.

◆ Create the space for bold dialogues to occur. This reduces anxiety and increases workers' sense of well-being, which, in turn, enhances productivity, engagement, and inclusion.

◆ ◆ ◆

Get Yourself Ready for Bold, Inclusive Conversations

Knowing others is intelligence;
knowing yourself is true wisdom.
Mastering others is strength;
mastering yourself is true power.

LAO TZU[1]

Chapter 1 focuses on the compelling business case for learning how to engage in bold, inclusive conversations. This chapter outlines what *you* need to do to get ready for the conversation. As highlighted in the preface, this is hard work. And the hard work begins with *you*. In the next chapter, I will delve into the importance of learning about those who are different from you as another key aspect of getting ready—also hard work.

A key reason for not being able to effectively dialogue about polarizing topics is our lack of cultural self-understanding. Bold conversations about race, religion, politics, and other polarizing subjects require different skills than other types of conversations. Historically we have not wanted to talk about these topics because it is just too hard, making us uncomfortable and often eliciting strong emotional responses.

I don't think we necessarily consider the ability to dialogue about race or other lightning-rod topics as a *real* skill, or at least not the way the dictionary defines the word as "difficult work." Our behaviors would suggest that we think we can expect individuals from vastly different world experiences to be able to sit together and discuss controversial and polarizing issues without the readiness and preparation to do so effectively. Getting yourself ready is a developmental process that involves learning to assess your current capabilities, understanding the gap between where you are and where you need to be for meaningful cross-difference dialogue. Readiness can actually take a long time because it is a skill that one develops over time through knowledge acquisition and practice.

The self-readiness steps include

- focusing on cultural self-understanding by exploring your **cultural identity**
- getting beyond "blindness"
- facing your fears and biases
- acknowledging the power in your power and privilege

EXPLORE YOUR OWN CULTURAL IDENTITY

We as humans must deal with an identity
located in the core of the individual yet also
in the core of our cultural community.

Erik Erikson, developmental psychologist[2]

Our cultural identity shapes our worldviews and, thus, all of the different opinions, attitudes, ideologies, and assumptions that we bring into our conversations.

Before you can have a bold conversation, you should engage in deep introspection. Any self-help book or leadership development program advises that the first step toward mastery is self-understanding. Introspection involves thinking about what you are thinking, a concept that behavioral scientists call metacognition.

Cultural self-understanding is a particular type of awareness that explores who you are culturally. Culture is bigger than any one of our identities. It is the combination of who we are and how we see and interpret the world. It may include our race/ethnicity, nationality, religion, geographic location, values, and beliefs. Our worldview is formed from our membership in a cultural community.

What Is Culture?

Culture can be defined as the behavioral interpretation of how a group lives out its values to survive and thrive, or, alternately, the unwritten practices, rules, and norms of a group. Most often, we take our culture for granted. It just *is*. However, our culture drives our behavior. Do we believe in shaking hands, bowing, or kissing when we meet someone new? Is it okay to show your emotions, or does your cultural norm say it is preferred not to be emotionally expressive when you are passionate or even angry about something? What does assertiveness look like in your culture? Is it a positive or negative attribute? It is not until we find ourselves out of our cultural norm that we recognize our own unique cultural patterns.

If you are member of a **dominant group** (e.g., white, male, heterosexual), you may not have to come out of your cultural comfort zone very often. I often hear leaders and others in training sessions struggle with an exercise that explores their cultural identity. Some say, "I don't really have a culture." While others say, "I just never thought about it before," and in the end find the exercise very self-revealing. Everybody has a cultural connection. There is no such thing as a view from nowhere. We get our worldview from somewhere, and it is in uncovering where and how that we enhance our cultural self-understanding.

Intersectionality

Intersectionality is a critical concept in understanding our identity and adds to the complexity of self-understanding. An example of how intersectionality manifests is reflected in the experiences of the gay, Muslim, Middle Eastern employee who called out his multiple identities in Chapter 1. Intersectionality theory acknowledges the overlapping and interdependent nature of simultaneously being a member of several historically marginalized groups.

First introduced by Sociologist Kimberlé Crenshaw in 1989 in a critique of feminist and antiracism discourse, intersectionality challenged the effectiveness of gender and civil rights ideologies, which had traditionally excluded the unique experiences of black women.[3] For women of color, the compounding effects of belonging to multiple marginalized identities (e.g., black, woman, low socio-economic class) created a unique experience that was oftentimes overlooked in the inquiry into and development of solutions that sought to address race and gender issues. According to intersectionality, the context and degree to which we experience power or marginalization is influenced by the intersection of our varying identities.

Those who are part of multiple non-dominant groups may be more sensitive to and aware of their differences, and are perhaps uncomfortable colluding with the cultural "rules" of the dominant group that are unfamiliar. The cultural exercise below encourages self-understanding. The questions posed are, more often than not, easier for those who are part of non-dominant groups (e.g., people of color, LGBTQ, those from a different religious group) to answer.

However, whether in the majority or minority, it is important to increase your cultural self-understanding.

Ask yourself these questions:

◆ *Who am I culturally?*

Where did I grow up, and what was the culture of my community growing up?

What did I learn about right/wrong, good/bad growing up?

What are my values and beliefs, and how have they changed over time?

If I had to describe a cultural community to which I belong, what would I say?

◆ *What is my cultural identity?*

Race/ethnicity

Generation

Religion

Education

Profession

Political persuasion

How does my cultural identity shape who I am and how I think?

◆ *What is my mindset about difference?*

Are we basically all the same as humans?

Are we more alike than we are different?

Is color blindness/gender blindness the best way?

Do I think my group's cultural norms are better than other people's?

Are differences normal, inevitable, something to learn about?

Gaining cultural self-understanding is not necessarily intuitive, especially for those in the dominant group. It takes time. Spend time with yourself understanding who you are.

Seek a partner, perhaps a family member or a trusted friend, who can help you on the journey.

GETTING BEYOND "BLINDNESS"

When someone says to me, "I don't see you as a black person," I interpret that as them not seeing me for who I am—that they don't see this core aspect of my identity (being black) as important. While I recognize that most people who make this statement mean well, they are saying that they see me as the same as them—I am their equal. They are, in effect, minimizing my difference. The reality is, I am different. To have bold, inclusive conversations, we must first acknowledge that there are important differences that make a difference.

Since the passage of the **Civil Rights Act of 1964**, when it became illegal to discriminate based on race, ethnicity, nationality, gender, and religion, we have focused on treating people the same, being color blind, gender blind, or blind to any differences. The legislation says that we should treat people equally. However, *equal* and *the same* are not synonymous. Many strive to practice the Golden Rule (treating others the way *you* want to be treated), rather than the **Platinum Rule** (treating others the way *they* want to be treated). You will not know how others want to be treated unless you have some level of understanding about others. Operating from the assumption that you know what is good for others because you know what is good for you can thwart efforts for mutual understanding.

The Golden Rule is a good starting point, but bold conversations are much more effective if you have the capability to practice the Platinum Rule. If we assume that we are basically all the same and minimize our differences, we have no incentive to spend time learning about others who may be from a different race, sexual orientation, ethnicity, and so on, because we feel there is essentially nothing to learn.

FINDING COMMON GROUND

A "sameness" mindset, however, can be a good place to start when there are polarized views. You want to find the common ground, a place of agreement from which to start the conversation. For example, we all want our communities to be safe, or we all want the best for our children. However, we may have different worldviews of how to accomplish these goals. Discovering our commonalities builds trust and an opening for deeper dialogue.

When we are polarized, the human tendency is to judge. We are so entrenched in our own beliefs, it sends us to our own corners, rather than to a place of non-judgmental curiosity about why we have different views. For example, white people may be more likely to hold the worldview that police officers are our friends. Based on experience, minority communities, particularly black communities, may have learned the exact opposite. To have bold conversations we have to explore our similarities (e.g., we all want our communities to be safe) before we can effectively talk about our differences.

My sister-in-law is Muslim. For many years, we did not talk about religion. While I respected and loved her very much, I had no knowledge of Islam. I thought it to be a very different religion from my own Christian beliefs and quite frankly I was afraid to ask questions because I did not want to appear ignorant. I felt we were polarized and it was best not to talk about it until one day in a conversation she mentioned Abraham, Isaac, and Jacob. I was stunned. I did not think that Islam would have any of the same Christian characters that I was familiar with. My point is that it was not until we found common ground—something that was the same—that we were able to continue to share commonalities and eventually begin to explore our differences.

"Going Along to Get Along"

Often, individuals from historically marginalized groups minimize their differences, or take a "go along to get along" stance, as a means of survival, which, in effect, can validate the "we are all the same" worldview. People with visible differences from non-dominant groups may find that to be successful they have to accentuate their similarities and downplay their differences. Differences may make majority group members uncomfortable. This dynamic makes it even more difficult to engage in meaningful conversations. Dominant group members may over-assume similarities, and minority group members might feel a need to understate differences. These two dynamics void each other out and result in no progress on really understanding the perspective of the other.

Bold conversations can happen only when there is an openness to acknowledge that there are differences that make a profound difference in perceptions and outcomes for many of us.

Stereotype Threats

A stereotype threat, a term coined by Claude Steele, is the expectation or the fear that one will be judged based on a negative stereotype about one's social identity group, rather than on actual performance and potential.[4]

Stereotype threats have been proven to have an immediate impact on performance. One study on stereotype threats and women's performance in math found that women are more likely to perform just as well on math tests as their male counterparts when the test is described as not producing gender differences in performance.[5] This condition countered the stereotype that women do not do as well in math as men.

Similar results were found among African American students on standardized tests.[6] Steele's study found that African American students were less likely to perform well when the test was described as diagnostic of intellectual ability. Even if the test was not an ability diagnostic, black students underperformed due to their fears of colluding with stereotypes that suggest blacks are intellectually inferior. They performed better when the test was described as non-diagnostic.

Although there are numerous laboratory studies in academic settings that show the impact of stereotype threats on performance, the influence in work settings has not been explored very much.

In a paper in *The Counseling Psychologist*, the authors explore the impact of stereotype threats at work. The authors contend that in a workplace where an individual is in the minority, there is a greater likelihood that this individual will experience stereotype threats. They posit that there are three potential responses to stereotype threats in the workplace:[7]

- *Overcompensation*—To prove that the stereotype does not apply to them or that they are not a typical member of their group, people may distance themselves from the negatively stereotyped group and assimilate by trying to behave and act more like those in a more positively viewed group. This is akin to minimizing their differences, the "go along to get along" phenomena.

- *Discouragement*—When an individual believes that no matter how hard he/she tries, the stereotype is just too big to overcome, this can manifest in disengagement from negative evaluations about one's group in order to preserve self-esteem. For example, from a psychological perspective, negative performance evaluations are discounted by the individual and not deemed relevant to his/her self-perception. In the short term, disengagement may work in preserving one's self-esteem, but in the long term, it may negatively impact motivation and performance because individuals believe they have no control over the outcomes.

◆ *Resiliency*—The authors believe many underrepresented groups actually manage to be resilient to stereotype threats in the workplace. It may play out in an advocacy or champion role, as one who supports learning and training in the organization to alleviate stereotypes. Other responses in this category include pointing out positive attributes of the targeted identity group and collective action, such as affinity groups that work to support inclusive practices.

It is important to understand the role of stereotype threats in developing the capability for bold, inclusive conversations. If the stereotype threats of "less intelligent" or "less articulate" are unconsciously playing out, it will certainly impact the effectiveness of the dialogue.

IDC Helps Us Understand How We Experience Difference

A useful model for assessing how we experience difference is the **Intercultural Development Continuum** (IDC), which is assessed by the Intercultural Development Inventory (IDI), developed and owned by IDI's president, Dr. Mitchell Hammer.

The theory is that as our experience with difference expands, we have a greater capacity to understand and bridge the complexities of cultural differences. It is a developmental model that contends that we advance through stages of greater capability to meaningfully address differences. Figure 2 highlights the developmental stages.

If we have had no experience with difference, we might be at the first stage, **denial**, where one would avoid or be disinterested in differences. The next stage is **polarization**, where we judge differences. Both denial and polarization are early

Intercultural Development Continuum

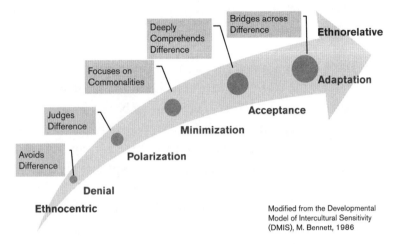

FIGURE 2. INTERCULTURAL DEVELOPMENT CONTINUUM

developmental phases where we have little experience or knowledge of differences and can see difference only through our own cultural lens (i.e., an **ethnocentric worldview**). When we are at polarization, the goal should be to move to **minimization**. The theory is that you must move through each stage as you develop cultural competence.

The third stage is minimization. This is where we practice the Golden Rule. Here, the mindset is that we are essentially all the same and any differences are inconsequential because we are all human. Minimization is where most people fall on the continuum because we have essentially been taught to minimize differences. As mentioned above, historically marginalized groups often minimize their differences as a way to "go along to get along." Individuals from dominant group identities minimize when they do not have a deeper comprehension of differences. Minimization can be a good place to find common ground but is insufficient for bold conversations.

The two stages that reflect a much deeper understanding of difference—a recognition that there are differences that make a difference and the need for those differences to be understood and bridged—are **acceptance** and **adaptation** (**ethnorelative** stages). At these stages, one embodies a more complex way of experiencing difference and is able to view the world from the perspective of other cultures. *Acceptance* does not mean *agreement*. It means that we accept that there are a number of ways that cultures experience the world and that we are curious to learn more about our differences. At the adaptation stage, not only do we recognize patterns of differences in our own and other cultures, but we also know how to effectively bridge those differences in mutually respectful ways. The Intercultural Development Inventory (IDI), a 50-question online psychometric inventory, is effective in providing a baseline of your individual (or group's) cultural competence, enhancing your self-understanding, and ultimately, gauging your readiness for bold, inclusive conversations (www.idiinventory.com).

FACE YOUR FEARS AND CHOOSE COURAGE

It takes courage . . . to endure the sharp pains of self-discovery rather than choose to take the dull pain of unconsciousness that would last the rest of our lives.

Marianne Williamson, *A Return to Love: Reflections on the Principles of* A Course in Miracles[8]

There is always some level of fear when you delve into unknown territory. Bold conversations require venturing outside one's comfort zone, which can be intimidating. The role of cultural identity makes dialogue even more complicated, because our identity groups are linked to a broader historical and social context. Sometimes history is uncomfortable and traumatic, which can make some of us fearful of having these discussions and more inclined to want to forget (or even deny) the past. For example, dialogue around race usually elicits fear and discomfort, largely due to the history of racism and the historical oppression of people of color. It is much easier for many to see these ills as isolated moments from the past. However we cannot forget or deny them because the intolerance, bigotry, and hatred have not disappeared. Anti-Semitism, Islamophobia, racism, and homophobia are still modern-day issues that continue to divide, polarize, and lead to violence and senseless killings. Instead of avoiding these conversations, we must identify strategies that alleviate our fears and position us to effectively engage in bold conversations as a means to solve these menacing problems.

Let's pause here. Do you experience a sense of fear when engaging in bold conversations? If so, ask yourself *what am I afraid of?* These questions are relevant whether you are a member of a dominant or non-dominant group. Are you afraid . . .

- of offending?
- of not knowing enough about the subject?
- of the conflict that might arise?
- of remembering some negative outcome from a previous dialogue?
- that you will be judged?
- that the other person won't "get it"?
- of the possibility of becoming emotional or angry?

As part of your self-discovery process, really probe why you might be afraid of having a bold conversation. Try to lean into your discomfort. Most things that are hard create some level of discomfort. By the same token, facing the difficulty and working through it brings satisfaction in the end.

It takes courage to face our fears. A 2012 *Psychology Today* article highlights six attributes of courage: (1) feeling fear, yet choosing to act; (2) following your heart; (3) persevering in the face of adversity; (4) standing up for what is right; (5) expanding your horizons and letting go of the familiar; (6) facing suffering with dignity and faith.[9] Practice finding your courage to have bold, inclusive conversations.

Along with courage, we need cultural humility to engage in conversations across difference. A 1998 article in the *Journal of Health Care for the Poor and Underserved* describes cultural competence in clinical training as a detached mastery of a theoretically finite body of knowledge. Cultural humility, on the other hand, incorporates lifelong commitment to self-evaluation and self-critique, to redress the power imbalances in the patient/physician dynamic.[10] Cultural humility is the ability to maintain an interpersonal stance that is other-oriented (or open to the other) in relation to aspects of cultural identity that are most important to the other person.

WE ALL HAVE BIASES

We all have biases, but most of us are unaware of how they manifest in our decisions and interactions. This is because social scientists assert that most of our biases are unconscious, and our unconscious biases drive 99 percent of our behaviors. **Unconscious bias** is a bias that happens automatically and is triggered by our brain making quick judgments and assessments of people and situations, influenced by our background, cultural environment, and personal experiences. How can you address your unconscious biases if you are unaware of them?

Know Your Culture: Increase self-understanding as discussed earlier. Know your own culture, why you believe what you believe, your history, and early experiences that have shaped your value system.

Change, Expand the Story: If unconscious biases are built up over time by the mind ingesting biased, partial, and negative messages, then the work to undo them is in meeting these messages with positive, affirming, counter-narratives that are equally powerful. Counter-narratives are only possible when you know what they are. If you don't know other stories, you cannot change the one that is in your head.

Nigerian novelist Chimamanda Adichie, in a compelling TED Talk called "The Danger of a Single Story," cautions that if we hear only a single story about another person or country, we risk stereotyping and vast misinterpretations.[11] In her talk, she says if the single story of Africa is that it is an undeveloped, poverty-ridden continent, you miss the other stories, like hers—growing up in a middle-class household with college-professor parents; or the rich history of a place like Timbuktu, the home of the first university in the world. What stories do you have about individuals, groups, and cultures that are different from yours? Is it a single story, or do you have several narratives in your mind—some perhaps good, others not so good, but a balance?

Describe before You Interpret: I do an exercise with clients in which I show a short video depicting the following interaction.

A man and woman walk silently into the room, never speaking, and the woman walks in behind the man with her eyes looking slightly downward. The man is wearing shoes and the woman is barefoot. The man comes to a chair and sits down, and then the woman sits on the floor next to him. The man acts like he's eating something from a bowl. He then passes the bowl to the woman, and she eats from the bowl. When she's finished, the man puts his hand just above the woman's bowed head—it looks as though he's almost pushing her head up and down—though his hand never actually touches her head. Then, the man stands up and leaves first, and the woman leaves behind him.

I ask them what they see. Words like subservience, male dominance, and gender inequality always surface—which are judgments and interpretations, rather than descriptions or observations. After that, I explain what is really happening in the video. "In the scene you just saw, the woman and the Earth are actually the two most sacred and revered aspects of their specific culture, so much so, that only the woman is holy and good enough to sit on the ground and touch it with her feet. Men can only experience the Earth through the woman. The man is charged with testing the food before it is proven fit for the woman; in case it is poisoned, he would die first. He is also charged with walking in first to deflect any attacks, and thus, to safely lead the way for her to walk unharmed."

Next I ask, "How did you see subordination, subservience, gender inequality?" Had they actually described their observations, they would have said "The woman had her head lowered" or "She was barefoot." However, their interpretations were based on what those behaviors mean for them. I follow up with the question "Where do our interpretations come from?" and the group recognizes that our unconscious biases direct our interpretations.

The Winters Group has developed a tool called DNA that supports us in being more intentional in naming and challenging our interpretations. DNA stands for **D**escribe, **N**avigate, **A**dapt.

DESCRIBE: Neutral description without judgment

Man and woman enter room. Man leads; Woman follows with her head down. Woman is barefoot. Man eats first.

NAVIGATE your interpretations		Alternate Interpretation #1 Subservience	Alternate Interpretation #2 Protection	Alternate Interpretation #3
Evaluate how you feel about each interpretation	Positive		It is wonderful that the man is protecting the woman	
	Negative	I don't like it		
How might you **ADAPT** based on your interpretation?	Choice or Decision #1	Speak out against gender inequality	Learn more about cultural differences	
	Choice or Decision #2			

FIGURE 3. THE WINTERS GROUP DNA TOOL
(Adapted from D.I.E., Kappler and Nokken,1999.)

Describe: First describe the behaviors and actions you see. Be careful not to let your personal judgments influence what you observe.

Navigate: Navigate your understanding. Be aware that your interpretations are influenced by the behaviors of your culture. What are alternative interpretations?

Adapt: Once you feel you have a pretty good understanding of the behaviors and actions you observed, begin to think of ways to navigate the situation effectively using mutual adaptation skills.

I ask participants to think of alternative interpretations via the DNA tool. Figure 3 is an example of how one might approach alternative interpretations using the earlier video, laying out the steps of describing without judgment, navigating and evaluating interpretations, and articulating possible adaptations. If your interpretation of the behaviors is "subservience," you would likely evaluate that negatively. If, however, your interpretation is that the man was protecting the woman, your evaluation and how you would adapt might be very different.

The DNA tool is useful in helping us to see beyond the single story (adapted from Nam & Condon, 2010).[12]

ACKNOWLEDGE YOUR POWER AND PRIVILEGE

Power and privilege determine who is invited to the table, who has access, and who can make decisions. Power also refers to the ability of individuals or groups to induce or influence systems and the beliefs or actions of other persons or groups. One's level of power or access to power is largely dependent on one's social status and group membership in various social categorizations, including race, class, sex, sexual orientation, gender identity/expression, age, religion, nationality, immigrant status, ability, and weight.

Privilege, at its essence, refers to the advantages that people benefit from based solely on their social status. It is a status that is conferred by society and perpetuated by systems that favor certain groups. This status is not necessarily asked for or appropriated by individuals, which is why it can be difficult for people to see their own privilege.

Power and privilege are relative. We all have it to a certain extent in different situations. However, from a systemic view, dominant groups in society have benefitted the most from unearned power and privilege. As you think about bold, inclusive conversations, consider, regardless of whether you are from the dominant or non-dominant group, what power or privilege you may have. For example, you may be a person of color—a group that has historically been without power and privilege—but in this situation, you are the manager, which puts you in a position of power from which to act.

Historically marginalized groups need to understand and

recognize the impact of power and privilege without blaming dominant group individuals for this condition. No effective conversation comes from the blame game. Power and privilege is systemic and complex. I also want historically marginalized groups not to automatically think they are powerless. I too often hear the sentiment: "What can I do? White people hold all of the power." You can change your perspective and definition of power. Power does not have to be a zero-sum game. It can mean shared power. We can see it as infinite. In his book, *Power: The Infinite Game,* Michael Broom contends that the infinite perspective of power means that we see the end goal as not winning or losing but rather as continuing the game and maintaining it.[13]

A finite perspective of power leads to a defensive stance where deception and secrecy are the preferred strategies. When we think of power as infinite, it evokes cooperation and openness. Bold, inclusive conversations happen only with an infinite power worldview.

Dominant group individuals should work on understanding the impact of their unearned power and privilege. Nondominant groups should not use that as a crutch but rather change their mindset, and, consequently, their behavior will change. If you see yourself as powerless, you act powerless. If you see yourself as having infinite power, you press on with confidence and resolve.

Here are some general, then more specific, questions that you should ask yourself about power and privilege, as part of your readiness to have a bold conversation.

- What is my positional power in this situation?
- Do I have power simply because I am a member of a dominant group?
- What influence do I have over the outcomes?

- If I am not a member of the dominant group, does the power and privilege of those who will be a part of the conversation concern me?

- As a member of the non-dominant group, what power do I have in this situation? Do I see power as finite or infinite?

- Can I essentially live being unaware on a day-to-day basis of my identity group (e.g., race, gender, sexual orientation, immigrant status)?

- Is it likely that I will be ostracized by my friends and family because of my sexual orientation?

- Can I demonstrate my religious beliefs without fear?

You should explore these and a host of other questions about power and privilege as part of your readiness to have a bold conversation. This mention of power and privilege just scratches the surface. I advise that you do some more research to gain a deeper understanding of this phenomena. It is at the core of our social issues, fuels polarization, and precludes the possibility of equitable dialogue.

If those involved are not ready for the complex discussions around power and privilege conversations, the result can be deeper polarization. It is not the first place you want to start if the participants are fairly new to having these types of conversations and there is a great deal of polarization.

CHAPTER 2 ◆ TIPS FOR TALKING ABOUT IT!

- **Remember that the ability to engage in bold, inclusive conversations is a journey that requires cultural self-understanding, addressing our biases and fears, and understanding our power and privilege.**

◆ Know your culture. Everybody has a cultural identity that shapes their worldview. We don't always consciously realize how our culture informs our perceptions and behavior.

◆ Resist the tendency to minimize differences. We tend to minimize our differences and overstate our similarities, leading us to practice the Golden Rule rather than the Platinum Rule.

◆ Resist the single story. Many of us only have a single story about those who are different. Meaningful dialogue will occur only if we learn more than one story about others.

◆ Take the Intercultural Development Inventory (IDI). It is a useful tool for assessing our readiness for bold, inclusive conversations.

◆ Recognize your power and privilege. Power and privilege are key determinants in the nature and tenor of cross-difference dialogue.

◆ Know your level of readiness before you engage in bold, inclusive conversations.

THREE

Expand Your Understanding of Others and Assess Organizational Readiness

Invite people into your life who don't look like
you, don't think like you, don't act like you,
don't come from where you come from, and
you might find that they will challenge your
assumptions and make you grow as a person.

MELLODY HOBSON[1]

The work to get ready for bold, inclusive conversations is personal, and it also requires assessing organizational readiness. Chapter 2 focused on the self-understanding aspect of readiness. This chapter highlights the importance of learning about other cultures as well as assessing organizational readiness.

In her 2014 TED Talk, "Color Blind or Color Brave?" Mellody Hobson, president of Ariel Capital, challenges us to venture outside our comfort zones, be intentional in engaging with our "others," and leverage difference, not only for the greater good but also for maximum business impact. Let's explore why having a greater understanding of other cultures or being "color brave" is so critical to engaging in bold, inclusive conversations.

CHALLENGE SINGLE STORIES

Historically we have not had much practice interacting across difference. In some cases, there were legal restrictions that prohibited cross-cultural interactions. For example, segregation laws kept black and white people from intermingling. Likewise, members of the LGBTQ community were forced to suppress that aspect of their identity until the last several decades. Historically, our norm has been not to express political views, and many of us were taught that religious beliefs that differed from our own were "wrong."

Readiness requires a level of knowledge about differences that goes beyond your worldview. It means that you have done some study on the issues, you have listened to different perspectives, even those contrary to your own, to give you a more balanced view. As mentioned in Chapter 1, social media gives us the ability to broaden and diversify our networks. However, we typically connect only with those who are most like us. Learning to engage in meaningful dialogue across difference requires not only understanding your view but also understanding what others believe and why. This is sometimes referred to as being able to walk in another's shoes, or empathy.

Many of us have only a single story about those who are different from us, as discussed in Chapter 2. We lack a wider worldview than what we get from those closest to us. We may be fearful of learning more because we have been taught not to talk about race, politics, and other issues, especially in the workplace. The Public Religion Research Institute (PRRI) included several questions on its 2013 American Values Survey designed to gauge the range and diversity of Americans' social networks. The survey results include the following:

♦ Seventy-five percent of white Americans reported that the circle of people with whom they "discuss important matters" is entirely white and only 15 percent said they have a racially mixed social network. Political affiliation made no difference in the results.

- Eighty-one percent of white Republicans and 78 percent of white Democrats have social networks that are entirely composed of whites. Among white independents, 73 percent say their social networks are comprised entirely of people who are white.

- Almost two-thirds (65 percent) of black Americans report having a social network comprised only of black people. However, 23 percent of black Americans answered that their network includes a mix of people from other racial and ethnic backgrounds, a percentage somewhat higher than that of white Americans.

- In contrast, only 46 percent of Hispanics report that their social networks are limited only to other Hispanics, and 34 percent report having a mixed social network.

- There were no gender differences and only slight differences by age. White Americans aged 65 and older were only slightly more likely than white young adults (ages 18–29) to have entirely white social networks (80 percent vs. 72 percent).[2]

In another survey, 56 percent of Americans think that Muslim values are at odds with American values. When asked, however, how often they have talked with a Muslim in the past year, 68 percent said never or seldom.[3] We certainly can't have meaningful dialogue across differences if we are not having any cross-difference contact at all.

The idea of integrating our schools and our neighborhoods is based on the premise that there are advantages to cross-cultural interactions. If we get to know each other better through more exposure and experience with each other, we break down the barriers and can more effectively explore our similarities and differences. As a matter of fact, George Romney, Mitt Romney's father, was a passionate supporter of integrated housing in the '60s. He said, "We've got to put an end to the idea of moving to suburban areas and living only among people of the same economic and social class."[4] Needless to say, that was not a popular worldview at the time, nor is it today.

PRACTICE THE 4Es

A critical aspect of being ready to have bold conversations about polarizing subjects is to have some knowledge of those who come from a different cultural community than your own. For this to happen, I offer the 4Es—**Exposure**, **Experience**, **Education**, and **Empathy**.

1. Exposure

An impactful exercise called Who's in My World invites participants to consider their own identity and the identity of those with whom they most often associate. For example, if I identify as black, and most of the people in my world are also black (e.g., people who regularly visit my home, people I socialize with, people in the movies I see and books that I read, my close friends, people in my faith community), I am getting very little opportunity for exposure to difference. If we don't have cross-group exposure, the likelihood of expanding our understanding of others is limited. Who's in your world?

2. Experience

Experience with difference is not the same as exposure. Diversity can be all around you without you ever really creating meaningful relationships and mutual understanding. Experience is about engaging with those who are different from you in ways that are cross-culturally enriching. Forging such relationships means that you are willing to address your fears, be vulnerable, and shed single-story narratives.

AT&T CEO Randall Stephenson's story about his lack of knowledge of his black friend's life experience discussed in Chapter 1 is a poignant example of how we can have exposure to difference without a meaningful experience. Developing cross-cultural relationships takes time, energy, and desire.

It may be more difficult for employees who think they have little in common to develop meaningful relationships. For instance, let's say the manager is a white male and the employee is a Southeast Asian woman. Finding commonalities to begin to connect and develop a meaningful work relationship that demonstrates that the manager cares about her as a person—and not just a production unit—may not be easy for either party. However, it is critical to engagement and retention, and vital in preparing for bold, inclusive conversations. Sharing meaningful experiences might include external team-building events, a work book club that allows different perspectives on the content, time in team meetings for members to talk about their culture.

One of the key drivers of engagement, according to Gallup's Q^{12} Engagement Survey is "somebody cares about me at work."[5] Gallup further asserts that it is important for employees to have a sense of belonging, which means feeling included. A study conducted by the Center for Talent Innovation, "Vaulting the Color Bar: How Sponsorship Levers Multicultural Professionals into Leadership," showed that 40 percent of African Americans and one-third of people of color overall feel like "outsiders" in their corporate culture, versus 26 percent of white employees who feel that way.[6] Bold, inclusive conversations will only be successful if employees feel that they belong, that they are cared about, and that their voices will be heard.

Encourage Reciprocal Learning

If you didn't grow up like I did then you don't know, and
if you don't know it's probably better you don't judge.

Junot Díaz, *The Brief Wondrous Life of Oscar Wao*[7]

The need to expand our knowledge about the other is mutual. The Winters Group offers a program called Cross-cultural Learning Partners, which aims to foster **reciprocal learning.** We pair individuals who are different in some way (e.g., race, gender, sexual orientation, religion) and invite them to go on a guided journey of learning about each other. This includes short lessons with reflective questions and recommendations for experiences that they can share (e.g., engage with each other's faith community or visit a cultural museum together).

The Cross-cultural Learning Partners program is grounded in the reciprocal nature of the learning, unlike many one-way mentoring programs, such as **reverse mentoring**, a very popular concept in today's workplace. Reverse mentoring programs are designed so that the person who is a member of the dominant group identity can learn more about the individual who is part of the non-dominant group. One-way programs perpetuate an "us-and-them" environment, and can contribute to polarization. Cross-cultural learning is specifically designed so that both parties are learning from each other, reducing the feeling that it is one-sided.

Historically marginalized groups need to learn about the majority as much as the majority needs to learn about marginalized groups. However, I contend that the historically marginalized groups may have a head start on this journey because our exposure, experience, and education has largely been from the dominant group perspective.

3. Education

Enhancing your exposure and experience is part of your education. However, those two Es need to be augmented with more formal education around difference. This can happen via workplace training, advanced university courses, movies, documentaries, museum visits, books, travel, and so on.

Beware of media reports as the only source of education about difference. We know that most reporting is biased, but beyond that, it may not provide a contextual understanding of the facts.

The Center for Racial Justice Innovation (Race Forward), compiled a report in 2015 called the Race Reporting Guide.[8] Geared toward helping journalists, the guide asserts that most race reporting focuses on individual, specific incidents or events and fails to include a broader context, such as the role of history, institutional policies, and inequitable practices; and it rarely features much coverage of racial justice advocacy or solutions. The report calls for a more systemic analysis that looks at root causes and the mechanisms that feed into patterns.[9]

The report also asserts that language matters. The words we use can be triggers (see Chapter 7 for examples of triggers) or paint stereotypical pictures. For example, terms like "illegal immigrants" should not be used. "Illegal" should be used to describe an action and not the person. Understanding both the role of language and the significance of educating oneself on broader contexts are critical to preparing for bold, inclusive conversations.

Let's Stop Punishing

There is a tendency to want to punish people, especially public figures, when they say something that offends a particular group. This results in a lot of media coverage and calls for their resignations, or worse; and when the action is taken against this obviously "bad" person (racist/sexist/homophobic, etc.), we all feel better again. But, what have we learned?

For those who may understand the reasons why the comments were inappropriate or offensive, the punishment is often warranted. For those who may not understand the context, it may have the effect of shutting down the possibility of conversations on polarizing topics. The fear of offending or not knowing enough can loom large in these situations, and unless people are inclined to dig deeper and do their own learning, they may alienate themselves from that group.

Juan Williams, a black journalist, was fired from NPR in 2010 when he said in an interview with Bill O'Reilly, "When I get on the plane, I got to tell you, if I see people who are in Muslim garb and I think, you know, they are identifying themselves first and foremost as Muslims, I get worried. I get nervous."[10]

Granted, as a public figure he probably should not have said that. However, he was probably articulating what a lot of Americans think (survey research would confirm that this is the case), and he was being honest. This could have been viewed as an opportunity to have deeper dialogue, to understand the underlying context with which the comments were made. It was an opportunity for education that was missed. If people think they will be punished for sharing honest fears and concerns, they will certainly not want to do so.

In a training session that I facilitated many years ago, a gentleman came up to me at the conclusion and said, "I got it . . . I just won't talk to any of my black coworkers. I don't want to offend anybody, and it is just better for me to keep my mouth shut." He obviously did not want to do the personal work required to learn more about differences.

There are certainly boundaries. There are certain comments or actions that deserve consequences (i.e., punishment). Many organizations have zero-tolerance rules that are explicitly spelled out in their Human Resources policies. I am not talking about those obvious, egregious comments that are mostly known to employees (e.g., racist, sexist, homophobic jokes; the "n" word). I mean the type of remarks that come from the I-don't-know-what-I-don't-know place on the learning curve. For example, it might be offensive if someone asks a black woman, "How did you get your hair like that?" or "May I touch your hair?" Rather than take offense, the black woman can use it as a learning opportunity to share with the person why such questions are offensive and inappropriate. If she assumes positive intent, the conversation is very different from the one that might have happened otherwise.

As I said earlier, we must cut each other some slack for bold, inclusive conversations to occur.

Ask yourself:

◆ Do I know the history of the other group from their perspective?

◆ Do I understand the underlying systems that impact outcomes for the group(s)?

◆ What do I know in general about cultural differences? (e.g., direct vs. indirect communication styles, individualistic vs. group-oriented cultures, how power is displayed, etc.)

◆ What do I know about their values and beliefs and how and why they were shaped as they are? (e.g., millennials' experience with technology differs from that of baby boomers, which shapes their worldview)

4. Empathy

Effective dialogue across difference will not happen if we cannot be empathetic. Empathy is not sympathy. Sympathy engenders pity. Empathy leads to mutual understanding and respect. It is encompassed in the theories of emotional intelligence, a concept that is now understood to drive personal and business success. Emotional intelligence is comprised of four parts: self-awareness, self-management, other awareness, and managing relationships. Emotional intelligence is a vital ingredient for effective bold, inclusive conversations.

Recognize Culturally Learned Communication Styles

While there are many cross-cultural differences that have been well researched and documented, the one that is most important to understand when having bold, inclusive conversations is how we have learned to communicate and handle conflict.

The **Intercultural Conflict Style Inventory**, developed by Dr. Mitchell Hammer, helps us to distinguish cultural preferences for solving problems and handling conflict. There are four preferred styles: discussion, engagement, accommodation, and dynamic, as shown below in Figure 4.

Discussion style is most preferred by Euro-American, Northern European, and Canadian cultures. It is characterized as direct and emotionally controlled. **Engagement style** is most commonly found among African Americans, Greeks, some Western Europeans, and some Latino cultures. Engagement style is direct and emotionally expressive. **Accommodation style**, preferred by many Asian cultures, is indirect and emotionally restrained. **Dynamic style**, common among Middle Eastern cultures, is indirect and emotionally expressive.

Those who prefer discussion style will advocate for logical, rational, fact-based arguments with limited emotional expressiveness, while those whose style is either dynamic or engagement-oriented will be comfortable with a strong display of emotion; they may be more apt to tell stories or

Intercultural Conflict Styles

	Discussion Style	Engagement Style
Disagreement by Verbal Direction	North America (e.g., US Canada, European American) Europe (e.g., Great Britain, Sweden, Norway, Denmark, Germany) Asia Pacific (e.g., Australia, New Zealand)	North America (e.g., African American) Europe (e.g., Greece, Italy, Spain) Central and Latin America (e.g., Cuba, Puerto Rico) Asia (e.g., Russia) Middle East (e.g., Israel)
Disagreement by Verbal Indirection	Latin America (e.g., Mexico, Peru) Asia (e.g., China, Japan, Thailand, Indonesia, Malaysia)	Arab Middle East (e.g., Kuwait, Egypt, Saudi Arabia, Lebanon) Asia (e.g., Pakistan)
	Accommodation Style	Dynamic Style
	Emotional Restraint	Emotional Expressiveness

(Left vertical axis label: How We Express Disagreement)

How We Express Emotion

FIGURE 4. INTERCULTURAL CONFLICT STYLES
(based on the Intercultural Conflict Style Model, M.R. Hammer, 2009)

use metaphors and circular reasoning. Someone who is prone to discussion style will use a more linear approach. Likely to prefer that people speak one at a time, discussion-style leaders may go around the room in a team meeting, asking everyone to speak in turn. Engagement-style leaders, on the other hand, may be more comfortable with over-talking and being interrupted.

I have coached several African American leaders who have received feedback that their passion (translation: display of emotion) needs to be contained. In one situation, the young woman was the highest ranking African American in the company. She was on the fast track. She developed a presentation about a very mundane compliance issue and decided to be creative in how she presented it. Rather than just sharing the facts, she developed a story about the topic using fictional characters.

After the presentation, she was under the impression that it had gone very well. However, a few days later, her manager shared that several of the senior leaders thought she should have just stayed with the facts. Her approach was inappropriate for the topic. At times, they said they thought they were listening to a Baptist preacher. This young woman's father, in fact, was a Baptist preacher and she acknowledged that unconsciously she may have mimicked some of his style. However, she was still hurt and frustrated because she felt even more alienated by her difference.

The Euro-American communication style relies heavily on logic and technical information rather than illusion, metaphor, and more creative and emotional styles of persuasion. Learning to communicate across cultures is a shared responsibility. In this case, if both had known more about culturally learned communication styles, the outcome may have been different.

Direct-communication cultures tend to be okay with voicing their unfiltered opinions and shooting from the hip, as the saying goes. Indirect cultures may be very uncomfortable speaking up without having had some reflection time or speaking before a senior leader has spoken. Disagreeing with one's superior might be considered disrespectful in some Asian cultures, whereas in discussion or engagement cultures, healthy debate is expected. Indirect cultures may not want criticism in public, whereas direct culture may be fine with public constructive feedback.

I have heard numerous times from Euro-American leaders that their Asian employees tend not to speak up in meetings. Often their solution is to force everyone to speak via round-robin techniques. This approach may be very uncomfortable for some Asian employees and those from other indirect cultures. When employees are reticent about speaking up in a meeting, discussion- or engagement-style leaders may interpret that they are not conversant on the topic or they are disengaged.

Using the concepts of the DNA model outlined in Chapter 2, consider alternate interpretations for the behavior. One alternate interpretation is that these employees have a different cultural norm for engaging. The solution might be to expand the number of approaches for soliciting input (e.g., one-one or electronic forms of communication) and not making it mandatory that everyone speak during a group meeting.

In a study conducted by Sylvia Ann Hewlett and reported in the *Harvard Business Review*, employees in a "speak-up" culture are 3.5 times as likely to contribute their full innovative potential.[11] However, we should consider alternative interpretations of what "speak up" means from a cultural perspective. It is critical, as part of your readiness for bold, inclusive conversations, to have a basic understanding of culturally learned communication styles.

A cautionary note: I do not want to stereotype different groups. Not all African Americans communicate engagement style; nor do all Asians prefer accommodation style. The explanation of the different styles is meant to help us understand that there are meaningful differences in how cultures communicate based on their norms, values, and beliefs. However, it does not mean that everyone who is a member of that group shares that characteristic. Some cultural groups, such as Native Americans, or Africans, may fall into any of the four styles, depending on factors including their history in terms of mobility and colonization.

BUILD CROSS-CULTURAL TRUST

There are myriad reasons for a lack of cross-cultural trust. Many historically marginalized groups have been taught not to trust the "other" based on historical atrocities, accounts of which have been passed down from generation to generation. "Never trust the white man" was a common admonition in my household growing up. I was also taught not to trust or associate with anybody who practiced a religion different from my own because they were surely going to hell. And according to my mother, Jewish people could not be trusted to be honest. How many of us come to the workplace with embedded "records" that may now be deep in our unconscious minds but nonetheless drive our perceptions and behaviors?

We don't have to rely on history to understand the lack of trust between majority and minority groups. There are numerous modern-day examples of why trust is limited. African American communities may not trust police because of their firsthand experiences with racial profiling. Women may not trust leadership to provide equal benefits and pay.

By the same token, majority-group members may not trust historically marginalized groups because they don't know them very well or because of the single-story phenomenon mentioned earlier that perpetuates stereotypes, such as a low intelligence, lack of motivation (e.g., blacks are lazy), and dishonesty (e.g., you can't trust Arabs).

One of the key readiness steps before embarking on bold, inclusive conversations is building trust. People will not talk honestly and openly when there is little or no trust. To build trust you need to consistently practice the 4Es as outlined above. Trust cannot be built without exposure to and experience with those who are different from you. How will you know when there is trust between two people or among the team? One key sign is the extent to which there is an openness to revealing and sharing personal information. Another sign of a trusting relationship is the willingness to be vulnerable—admitting weaknesses, acknowledging what you don't know.

Paul Zak's *Harvard Business Review* article, "The Neuroscience of Trust," explores a study that compared people at low-trust companies with people at high-trust companies. Those at high-trust companies report 74 percent less stress, 106 percent more energy at work, 50 percent higher productivity, 13 percent fewer sick days, 76 percent more engagement, 29 percent more satisfaction with their lives, and 40 percent less burnout.[12] He and his colleagues found through scientific brain studies and other research that there are eight management behaviors that foster trust. Four are particularly pertinent to fostering bold, inclusive conversations.

Share Information Broadly: If you do not have the whole picture (e.g., just a single story), it is impossible to have effective dialogue.

Intentionally Build Relationships: As mentioned above, exposure and experience with differences are critical components of bold, inclusive conversations. The better I know you, the more I can trust you. We tend not to develop relationships across race, ethnicity, disability status, sexual orientation in part due to the fear of the unknown and our human tendency to stay with our own tribe. Zak's research shows that when people intentionally build social ties at work, their performance improved. Finding common ground, as recommended in Chapter 2, can facilitate the ability to begin to build meaningful relationships across difference.

Show Vulnerability: The willingness on the part of leaders to admit when they do not know something builds credibility and trust, according to Zak's research. It may be more difficult to admit ignorance on topics like race and religion due to the fear of how it will look to the employee. Managers may feel as if they should know more than they do, and historically marginalized employees may feel the same. This is where patience and cutting each other some slack are important. When a manager genuinely shows interest and honestly admits to not knowing, it will likely engender more trust.

Facilitate Whole-Person Growth: We often define inclusion, in part, as the ability for individuals to bring their whole selves to work. Zak contends that assessing personal growth with discussions about work-life integration and family has a powerful effect on trust, as does allowing time for recreation and reflection, which improves engagement and retention. Leaders need to build skills to be comfortable talking about personal aspects with employees who are culturally different from them. I often hear from historically marginalized groups that such conversations are awkward. There is a shared responsibility. Members of historically marginalized groups need to develop skills for the more personal conversations as well. Finding common ground, discussed in Chapter 2, is a good place to start.

In Steven Covey's book, *Speed of Trust*, one of the core tenets of building trusting relationships is straight talk.[13] "Say what is on your mind. Don't hide your agenda. When we talk straight, we tell the truth and leave the right impression." While this may be sound advice, it doesn't work all of the time if you are from a historically marginalized group. Here are some reasons why straight talk is not always safe.

From the perspective of the historically marginalized group:

- "If I tell you exactly what it feels like to be a ＿＿＿ in this organization, you think I am whining or being overly sensitive."

- "Straight talk will make you feel guilty or ashamed, and I don't want to make you feel bad. It could be a career derailer."
- "I don't trust you with my straight talk. You would just not understand it, and I am not sure how you might share it or misinterpret it."
- "If I say what is on my mind, I might lose my job."
- "Nobody in this company really says what they think. I am not going to put myself out there."
- "I am not the spokesperson for my identity group. You may use my perspective to generalize my group."

From the dominant-group perspective:

- "If I was to talk straight to you, I would have to admit that I really don't know anything about your group. I am embarrassed to admit that."
- "I can't talk straight with you because you might get offended and file a lawsuit against the company."
- "Nobody in this company really says what they think. I am not going to put myself out there."

Trust is built differently across cultures. Thomas Kochman in *Conflict Styles in Black and White* posited that African Americans tend to build trust via sharing one's emotional reality in a direct manner and whites tend to build trust via controlling emotion.[14] He found that black people can trust you if you are straight with them and tell them exactly what you think and feel. He found that for whites, trust was built when you spare feelings to help keep the difficult conversation "on track."

Such differences need to be acknowledged and understood to build mutual trust across difference. Experts agree that it takes years to build trust, seconds to break it, and forever to repair it. Building trust is a process—a journey—and not an event.

IS IT FACT OR TRUTH?

There's a world of difference between truth
and facts. Facts can obscure the truth.

Maya Angelou[15]

Understanding the difference between fact and truth can help us to build trust. While it might seem like splitting hairs, I think it is important to call out the distinction. Some will say, "just the facts please." Others will say, "What is the truth about this situation?" A fact is something that is undeniable and will stand until proven wrong. It is universally accepted. It is something that has happened or occurred. For example, that the Louvre is in Paris is a fact. Truth is much more subjective, incorporating feelings and beliefs, and it can change. Something may be true for me—I am afraid of heights—but not true for you. Additionally I might not always be afraid of heights. It may be true now but not always.

The reason that this is an important distinction is because in dialogue we can erode trust if we judge one's truth. "It's silly to be afraid of heights" or "You need to get over that" would be judgments that could negatively impact conversation. One's perception of a situation is one's truth. Respecting another's truth is important. Understanding why something is true for that individual is necessary to engage in bold, inclusive conversations.

For example, if a woman thinks that she is not being taken seriously for her contributions, this might be considered her truth. This is what she experiences. She may have facts to substantiate her beliefs: incidences that have occurred— someone else got the promotion, for example. Her male boss thinks otherwise, based on his truth. The fact might be that over his career he has promoted a number of women. It does not change this woman's truth that she has not been promoted. It can be challenging to find common ground without sorting out the facts from one's truth and recognizing that they are both important.

SEPARATE THE PERSON FROM THE POSITION

President Barack Obama said we can disagree without being disagreeable. We can also oppose someone's perspective and not demonize that person. For example, we may read a post from a friend or colleague on Facebook about their political leanings with which we disagree, and we immediately judge the person rather than just judging the idea. When we agree with others, we judge them as intelligent and informed. However, when we disagree, our judgments of the person are negative. We may label them as racists or homophobic, based on their support of a particular candidate or position.

Developing the capability to judge one's idea without judging the person with that belief is really hard. During the 2016 presidential campaign there was a tendency by some Democrats to judge all Donald Trump supporters as bigots. Without knowing why someone supported one candidate or another, we cannot make broad judgments about their principles.

Be cautious about being too eager to be inclusive for the sake of inclusion. Sometimes there is a thin line between being inclusive of diverse versus harmful positions. The goal should not be to accept all positions, rather to be initially curious and open to understanding why one may take a particular position before totally judging the person.

As another example, pro-choice versus pro-life perspectives are very polarizing in this country. If you are pro-choice, can you respect a person who is pro-life? Can you disagree with someone's position without negatively labeling the person? If the person holding the pro-life viewpoint takes some action that is harmful to others (e.g., attempting to stop individuals from entering abortion clinics), you would have grounds for judging the person based on potentially harmful behavior and their refusal to allow others to exercise their rights. If, however, the person with the pro-life views exercises their beliefs as it relates to their own decisions and choices, and respects that others have the right to make different decisions and choices, perhaps we are then able to separate the person from the position.

ASSESS ORGANIZATIONAL READINESS

The notion of culture certainly extends to organizational culture. So far, I have advised you to enhance your understanding of your own cultural norms and frameworks as well as those of others. Understanding the organizational culture is also key in assessing readiness to engage in bold, inclusive conversations. How would you answer the following questions about your organization?

- Is inclusion explicitly articulated as one of the organization's values?
- Does the organization demonstrate that it values inclusion through actions by all leaders in the organization?
- Are there formal programs in place promoting inclusion (e.g., employee network groups, mentoring, training, recruitment of diverse talent, etc.)?
- Does the organization celebrate diversity with different company-sponsored events?
- Does the organization actively support philanthropic causes of diverse groups?

- Is there visible evidence of employee diversity?

- Are leaders evaluated on their inclusion practices?

- Is it a culture of risk taking or risk aversion?

- Is it common to call out the "elephants in the room" or does the organization tend not to tackle tough subjects?

- Would you characterize the culture as passive-aggressive?

- Do leaders show they care about all employees?

- Is the culture open or closed (i.e., few people allowed in the inner circle)?

- Are leaders well trained to support employee development and address relevant personal concerns?

- What is the level of trust of leadership?

If the culture does not demonstrate that it values all employees and incorporates inclusion as one of its core values, it may not be ready to tackle bold, inclusive conversations.

As part of the readiness process, one organization assembled a small task force to evaluate the content of the dialogue session against the organizational culture. The initial content was designed to focus primarily on issues of race. The team determined that while race needed to be addressed as its own issue, the organization was not ready to tackle race by itself. This initial session would be more successful, they concluded, if it was reframed to encompass other diversity dimensions. The title was changed from Workplace Trauma in the age of #BlackLivesMatter to Affirming Inclusion and Building Bridges during Challenging Times. Piloted with a group of HR and diversity leaders, the session was very successful, and the organization now plans to continue the dialogues, working up to discussing race, as well as a more comprehensive treatment of specific topics, such as LGBTQ and religion.

You may think that you are personally ready to have bold conversations on polarizing topics, and you may also think that your organization needs to engage in these conversations because it would help to create a more inclusive climate. However, the facts may suggest otherwise. Tackling these topics before the organization is ready could be disastrous, leaving those involved feeling more alienated and polarized. In Chapter 2, I introduced the Intercultural Development Inventory and the Intercultural Developmental Continuum, which reveals that most people have a minimization mindset. A bold discussion on race will likely be more successful with those who are at acceptance and adaptation on the continuum.

A session that is inclusive of different dimensions of diversity works well for those with a minimization worldview because they may view it as "treating everyone the same" and not focusing on one particular group. It was a smart move for this organization to recognize that it needed more development—both in self-understanding and in understanding other cultures—before delving into race, one of the most complex and divisive issues of our time.

ARE YOU REALLY READY FOR BOLD, INCLUSIVE CONVERSATIONS?

After reading Chapters 2 and 3, you might be thinking, *If I have to do all of this to get ready to have a bold, inclusive conversation, forget it. It is just too much work.*

Do not despair. If you have gotten through these chapters, you must have some level of interest in learning how to engage in bold conversations.

Chapters 2 and 3 simply highlight the imperative of ensuring that you are ready to engage in these difficult cross-cultural discussions and some of the important knowledge about others that is necessary. Readiness is a journey. You do not have to wait until you have mastered all of the readiness skills before you start to have conversations across difference.

At the very least, raise your self-awareness and your knowledge of the differences, as outlined in these two chapters, before attempting to engage in bold, inclusive conversations. You will need to acknowledge your skill level (e.g., "I am new at this," "I don't know as much as I need to know about our differences," "I am still learning and hope you will support me in that journey"). As proven by Zak's research highlighted above, showing your vulnerability and being willing to learn can go a long way in building trusting relationships.

Answer the self-assessment survey on page 64 to gauge your readiness for bold, inclusive conversations.

If you answered "somewhat" or "not at all" to *all* of the statements, you are definitely not ready to engage in polarizing conversations. If you answered "somewhat" or "not at all" to more than half of the statements, proceed with caution. If you were able to answer "a great deal" or "somewhat" to at least half of the statements, you can likely move more quickly through the steps that will be provided in Chapters 5 and 6.

Simultaneously work on your readiness and move cautiously into the conversations, being mindful of how far your readiness will take you. As this is a skill, do not go beyond your capabilities, and continue to enhance them so that you can enjoy increasingly mutually beneficial interchanges across differences.

You might be thinking, *How long will it take to get ready?* I really don't know. As you can see from the self-assessment, it depends on a number of different factors. The key point is, if

READINESS SELF-ASSESSMENT

		A great deal	Some-what	Not at all
1.	I am culturally self-aware.	☐	☐	☐
2.	I have explored my unconscious biases.	☐	☐	☐
3.	I am comfortable talking about difficult subjects.	☐	☐	☐
4.	I believe that treating everyone the same is not the solution to polarization.	☐	☐	☐
5.	I have studied my own and other culture's norms and beliefs.	☐	☐	☐
6.	I have a high degree of emotional intelligence.	☐	☐	☐
7.	I readily acknowledge that I don't know what I don't know.	☐	☐	☐
8.	I recognize that there are differences that make a difference and I try not to minimize them.	☐	☐	☐
9.	I have regular exposure to difference.	☐	☐	☐
10.	I have meaningful relationships with diverse individuals and groups.	☐	☐	☐
11.	I can separate the person from their position.	☐	☐	☐
12.	My organizational culture is ready to have bold, inclusive conversations.	☐	☐	☐
13.	There is a high level of trust in the organization.	☐	☐	☐
14.	There is a high level of trust within my team.	☐	☐	☐
15.	I am aware of my power and privilege.	☐	☐	☐
16.	I already have a lot of experience with bold, inclusive conversations.	☐	☐	☐

you are not ready, don't try to tackle the tough conversations. Go slowly and methodically. The remaining chapters provide guidance on the process.

CHAPTER 3 ◆ TIPS FOR TALKING ABOUT IT!

◆ Learn about those who are different. We may not have enough knowledge of cultural differences to effectively engage in bold, inclusive conversations.

◆ Learn to understand others from *their* worldview, not yours. Learning about others from their perspective (i.e., the ability to walk in their shoes) is key to forging mutual understanding.

◆ Remember that learning about others requires exposure, experience, education, and empathy.

◆ Engage in mutual or reciprocal learning. The need to expand our knowledge about the other is mutual.

◆ Recognize the importance of trust. Building trust across difference is a prerequisite to bold, inclusive conversations.

◆ Learn how cultures differ in their communication styles to engage in bold, inclusive conversations.

◆ As well as personal readiness, assess organizational readiness for bold, inclusive conversations.

◆ ◆ ◆

FOUR

Prepare: Why, Who, What, How, Where, and When?

By failing to prepare, you are preparing to fail.

BENJAMIN FRANKLIN

In Chapters 2 and 3, we explored readiness for bold, inclusive conversations. This chapter focuses on preparation. Readiness is the ongoing learning process of becoming more knowledgeable about yourself and those who are different from you, whereas preparation is the plan for an impending conversation. We explore the tactical aspects of preparing for the conversation in this chapter.

It is useful to use the Why, Who, What, How, Where, and When model often used in investigative reporting and other types of research as a template for getting prepared.

WHY ARE YOU HAVING A BOLD, INCLUSIVE CONVERSATION?

The most critical question to consider is *why* are we pursuing a dialogue about X?

◆ What is the main reason for this particular bold, inclusive conversation?

◆ Why is this an important conversation to engage in? Why is it important to you? Do you think it is just as important to others who you want to be a part of the conversation?

◆ Is there pressure from certain individuals or groups to engage in this dialogue?

◆ Is it a part of what the organization normally does when there are polarizing issues, or would this be an exception to your organizational cultural norms?

◆ Is this one-one performance feedback conversation?

◆ Is there a shared understanding of the purpose for the dialogue?

One organization decided to set up one-one conversations between senior leaders and employees of color. The impetus for these conversations stemmed from a realization that employees of color were not being promoted at the same rate as their white counterparts. Leadership concluded that this was because they did not know the employees of color very well. They decided that holding 30-minute, individual get-to-know-you meetings would be a good first step.

The leaders responded positively to these meetings, indicating that they had gone very well. In contrast, the employees of color were confused and in some cases anxious about the security of their jobs. Some asked, "Why am I having this session with a senior leader? Am I in trouble?" Others asked, "Why are you doing this now?" The stated purpose of "just wanting to get to know you" left the employees of color wondering why and why *now*. One employee of color noted, "You have not wanted to get to know me before."

There was no shared understanding of the purpose of the meetings, and it therefore resulted in skepticism and may have reduced trust in senior leaders on the part of employees of color.

It is critical to clearly communicate the *why* and to ensure that there is shared meaning.

WHO WILL BE INVOLVED IN THE CONVERSATION AND WHY?

◆ Will this be a one-one conversation, or will it involve a larger group?

◆ Who is convening the dialogue—leadership, the communications department, HR, the diversity and inclusion department, or an employee affinity group?

◆ Is it going to be formal or more of an informal conversation?

◆ If it is a group, will it be an intact team discussion, or will it be open to a larger group, many who may not know each other?

◆ Will all participants be on the same level in the organization, or will managers and supervisors be in attendance?

◆ What is the rationale for inviting or not inviting certain individuals or groups?

The Town Hall Example

In an attempt to quell fears and reaffirm its commitment to diversity and inclusion, an organization decided to have a town hall meeting to discuss some recent tragic events, including terrorist attacks and the killings of unarmed black men. The session was open to everyone. Inasmuch as this organization routinely held town hall meetings facilitated by the CEO or other senior leaders, there was good attendance from a cross-section of employees from different backgrounds and different areas of the company.

However, unlike other town hall meetings where employees readily engaged in the conversation, there was uncomfortable silence during this meeting. After the meeting, the organizers realized that employees were not willing to share their thoughts on these topics, recognizing how polarizing they are and being fearful that their opinions would be judged and criticized in front of leaders and coworkers.

Affinity Group Example 1

Another organization decided to take a different approach. I was invited to facilitate a two-hour session with the African American employee affinity group to discuss the stress that the killing of unarmed black men was causing among its members. The purpose of the meeting was twofold: share feelings and develop skills to effectively discuss these topics. Initially, the thought was to invite senior leaders who could hear the frustration and concern among the African American employees.

However, we decided that the first session might be more effective if it was confined to the affinity group members. This approach allowed for a more open dialogue than might have been achieved if the session had been open to leaders. The employees of this organization are quite dispersed, and while a number had independently shared their frustrations with the leader of the affinity group, there had not been an opportunity for members to hear from each other.

During this first session, it became apparent that there was a need for another session with just the African American employee affinity group because we were only able to accomplish the first objective of sharing feelings. I realized that the emotions were still so raw that it would not be prudent to try to work on the skill-building portion of the agenda.

During the second session, a recommendation surfaced to hold a third gathering that would include other employee network groups (e.g., Latino, Asian, LGBTQ), as well as members of the Diversity Council. This particular diversity council is comprised of some senior leaders in the organization. The purpose of the combined session was to be more inclusive and explore other issues that might be causing stress for these groups (e.g., fear of being deported, Islamophobia concerns). The third, combined session surfaced new issues, such as the gay, Muslim, Middle Eastern young man who voiced his fear of standing too close to the edge of the track at the Metro station for fear of being pushed, referenced in Chapter 1.

This was a meaningful dialogue in which we were able to talk about specific skills such as meeting people where they are (e.g., using the Intercultural Development Continuum model to assess the level of competency as outlined in Chapter 2); managing emotions, using "I" statements; and listening. Chapter 5 elaborates on these skills.

Affinity Group Example 2

A different organization had difficulty initially getting approval to hold a dialogue session with their African American affinity group employees. The leadership did not want to endorse a discussion about topics that had historically been discouraged in the workplace. Conceding that the proliferation of tragic events constituted extraordinary circumstances, the session was approved, but only if the most senior African American leaders were present and it was open to all employees.

I was invited to facilitate the session, and, as it turned out, only members of the African American network group chose to attend. The presence of African American senior leadership was very impactful. The highest-ranking African American leader was able to speak on behalf of all senior leaders. Employees were encouraged that senior leaders were there to listen. The group decided that this was the first in what should be ongoing dialogues about timely topics that may disrupt their ability to be totally present doing their best work.

There are pros and cons to including different levels within the organization in the sessions. On the one hand, when leaders are present, there is a greater likelihood that some type of action will result, if that is one of the goals. Additionally, leaders hear employees' perceptions firsthand. The disadvantage is that employees may be reticent to speak their mind in the presence of senior leadership. The key is knowing who to invite at what point in the conversation. That will depend on a number of factors, including readiness and the purpose of the meeting (e.g., just to raise awareness, listening, brainstorming, skill building). It will also depend on organizational norms (i.e., is it customary to hold multi-level meetings?).

Leverage Employee Affinity Groups

The impetus for the conversations referenced above came from employee affinity groups. Utilizing existing networks such as this can be very effective in organizing bold, inclusive conversations. Employee affinity groups are in tune with the issues facing their respective groups, have already been sanctioned by the company, and therefore have some level of credibility and leverage. A senior leader in the organization generally sponsors one or more of the organization's affinity groups.

Typically, the sponsor's role is to advise and support the group in achieving its goals. Network sponsors attended the various sessions that I have facilitated, which sent a very positive signal to the participants. In most cases, the sponsor opened the meeting with an overview of the importance of the conversation and shared a message that leadership wanted to ensure that all employees felt valued and included. The sponsor was in most cases from a different identity group (e.g., white men sponsored the African American network for the sessions I facilitated). The primary role during the conversation, stated by the sponsor, was to listen and answer any direct questions that participants might have.

If your organization does not have employee affinity groups, you may have a diversity council or committee, which can be very helpful in organizing bold, inclusive conversations. If there is no group that is already in place, well-respected senior leaders could be approached who might support such conversations.

Who Should Facilitate?

Another important *who* question is who will facilitate the session. Will it be an internal HR person or an external consultant? One client, the chief diversity officer of a large financial institution, decided to facilitate an open dialogue herself. While I was not there, she told me that it went very well. It was open to all employees, and over a hundred participated. The purpose of the dialogue was to raise awareness of the potential impact of the external tragedies on employees.

The advantage of an internal facilitator is that the person is likely well known in the organization, which might lead to a more candid dialogue. On the other hand, where I have been invited to facilitate, it is largely because I not only bring facilitation skills but also experience from other client settings and perhaps a more neutral, less threatening point of view.

It is critical for group sessions to engage an experienced facilitator to guide the session. Of course if it is a one-one session, there would be no need for a third party, unless the circumstances warranted it (e.g., the person asking for the bold conversation wants an advocate or ally in the room or there is need for translation or other accommodations).

WHAT IS THE EXPECTED OUTCOME?

The next question after *why* and *who* is, What do we want to achieve during this dialogue? Many of us are trained to move as swiftly as possible from problem identification to solutions. Topics such as race, religion, and politics are complex and do not lend themselves as easily to popular problem-solving models, such as assess, plan, do (take action), evaluate. This type of model is a good starting point for a dialogue framework. However, it should be expected that the assessment and planning parts may take longer and require more readiness than uncontroversial topics, such as how you will fix a software glitch. The situation mentioned earlier in this chapter about the company that decided to hold 30-minute one-one meetings as a means of getting to know employees of color is an example of not spending enough time on assessing and planning before getting to action.

Effective assessment requires readiness, and, as pointed out in Chapters 1 and 2, readiness takes time. Planning is akin to preparation, the focus of this chapter. The point here is that before you even think about the *do* part, take the time to adequately assess and plan. Many business people have been taught to be action oriented. (What are we going to do about this? We want to get to solutions as quickly as possible so we can get on with it or get to the next problem.)

Consider the short-term desired outcome as well as what you want to achieve in the longer term.

The short-term outcome of a bold, inclusive dialogue might simply be to listen and share perspectives. Ground rules for the first conversation might include no debating, no criticisms, and questions for clarification only. I learned very soon into the first session that my agenda was too full. There was no way in two hours that we were going to be able to listen and also do some skill building. I realized that this group just wanted and, quite frankly, just *needed* to talk, to share with each other how the events—such as the killing of unarmed black men and people being targeted because of their religion—were impacting them and their ability to stay focused on work. There should have been no other expected outcome for that initial session beyond sharing.

The *why*, *what*, and *who* for more dialogue sessions may organically unfold. In the example referenced above, the group decided during the second meeting that its members should expand their efforts to include additional employee affinity groups.

What? So What? Now What? Analysis

A useful tool for planning and developing an agenda of expected outcomes for each session is the framework that asks What? So what? Now what? Here is an example based on the situation described above.

- **What?** Hold a session to share feelings about recent tragic events.

- **So what?** Acknowledgment of similar emotional responses can be cathartic and validating, and as a result we feel better and can more easily concentrate on work.

- **Now what?** Expand our dialogue to include other affinity groups.

The agenda for each conversation should be written and provided to each participant. The agenda should clearly stipulate what will and will not be discussed during that particular conversation. However, I have found that cultures that are from the oral tradition of communication (e.g., African American, Latino, Native American), might not feel bound by the written agenda and will be more apt to let the conversation go where it goes. It is important to have a good facilitator who can steer the group back to the agenda or at least confirm that they want to change the agenda.

HOW WILL YOU ENGAGE IN A BOLD, INCLUSIVE CONVERSATION?

It is important to consider what methods will be used to convene a bold, inclusive conversation. Will the session(s) be in person, virtual, or some combination?

Pros and Cons of Virtual Gatherings

A virtual session includes a facilitator, just like the live session. Participants log in using their computers and are linked to the facilitator, the visual materials, and each other for the dialogue.

Initially, I doubted the effectiveness of this method. I was convinced that sensitive topics like race, religion, and politics could only be effectively addressed in face-to-face venues. However, I soon learned that most employees are now used to gathering virtually and are comfortable using this approach. They readily type their responses using the chat feature of the software. Even when we invite participants to speak their opinions using the phone feature, the vast majority choose to type in their comments.

One of the key advantages of virtual dialogue is that participants can remain somewhat anonymous depending on who is participating and how they identify themselves (e.g., full name, first name only, pseudonym). This can also be a disadvantage because some might feel that it gives them license to make disparaging, inappropriate comments. This rarely happens when it is an organization-sponsored session. However, during a public virtual webinar that we conducted immediately following the 2016 presidential election, we were forced to close the written chat comments because of some very negative comments and name-calling.

Another advantage of virtual sessions is that they can be pulled together very quickly because participants do not have to leave their workstations. This also alleviates time away from work, thereby mitigating lost productivity. However, this can also be a disadvantage inasmuch as participants may use the opportunity to multitask and not stay focused on the session. We try to account for this possibility by conducting lots of polls and interspersing many discussion opportunities during the session.

While virtual technology essentially allows us to do everything we would accomplish in face-to-face settings, including role-playing skill-building exercises, it has its drawbacks, including technology malfunctions. We use a lot of videos in our virtual meetings, and sometimes participants are frustrated because they are not able to view or hear them. The usual problem is software incompatibility.

In-Person Sessions

This traditional way of convening people may still be the most effective for bold, inclusive conversations. From a perception perspective, some people may feel that it is more personal and sends a signal that you care more about the topic/ issue. If you are willing to take the time and effort to meet with me in person, I think you care more.

Another advantage to meeting in person is the ability to assess tone and body language, which is not possible when using the chat feature of virtual methods. In-person sessions also more readily lend themselves to team and relationship building with groups who may not already know each other, especially if it is a session in which different levels of the organization are participating. Being able to see the leader might make it easier to speak up.

Initial sessions with the purpose of just listening or raising awareness can be successfully accomplished using virtual methods. However, when you get to the stages of really being bold in discussing polarizing topics, face-to-face is preferable.

Combining In-Person and Virtual Sessions

Some organizations use a combination approach because they have a large work-from-home workforce as well as people dispersed throughout the world. Telepresence technology is used to support these sessions, providing an effective simulated in-person experience for the remote participants. Some organizations have participants all gather in the same physical space, sharing the same on-line connection to the facilitator and materials.

WHERE SHOULD BOLD, INCLUSIVE DIALOGUES TAKE PLACE?

While this is not a concern for virtual sessions (except when participants come together in the same physical space), for in-person sessions, place matters. Consider the following when planning where it should take place:

◆ Is the room the right size?
◆ How is the room configured?
◆ What environmental concerns (heating, air conditioning) might there be?
◆ Is the space easily accessible?

Several of the places selected for in-person sessions that I have facilitated have been less than ideal. In one case the room was way too small, and in another, the room was way too big. One of the sessions was held in a large auditorium that probably seated 500 people. There were about 25 in attendance. It did not create a conducive atmosphere for open, inclusive dialogue. One time the room was freezing, and there seemed to be no remedy. Another session was in a room that was way too hot. One particular session was held in a room that was very hard to find. Many participants arrived late and just a bit frustrated.

While I recognize that many of the place considerations may be out of the control of those organizing the dialogue, I mention these items because, given the fact that the topic is already emotionally charged, you will want to manage as many of the logistical aspects as you can. The success of the meeting will be influenced by these factors. I have heard comments such as "They put us in the worst room possible—another sign that they just don't care. We are not that important" and "The room is so far away. I wonder if they did that on purpose, to discourage us from attending." When there is little trust or maybe even some paranoia, you will want to be proactive in considering how to alleviate such perceptions.

An ideal configuration for the room setup might be a circle of chairs with no table, or a U-shaped setup that allows participants to see each other. Theater-style arrangements might be too formal and require those who wish to speak to stand up, which might mean that their backs are to some participants. This might require them to come up to the front of the room, which might be uncomfortable for some. The configuration depends on the type of forum (e.g., town-hall style vs. smaller, more intimate gathering) and the purpose of the meeting. There is no one right answer. However, I recommend that you proactively consider room setup.

A planning template to assist in preparing for a bold, inclusive conversation is provided below.

PLANNING TOOL FOR BOLD, INCLUSIVE CONVERSATIONS

	Conversation 1
Why are we having this conversation?	
Who should be invited?	
What is the desired outcome? (Just listening, creating shared meaning, probing differences?)	
Where and when should we hold the conversation?	
Room set up (for in-person), technology needs	
How should the conversation be conducted? (In-person, virtual)	
How many sessions are anticipated?	
Who will facilitate the session?	

Conversation 2	Conversation 3	Conversation 4

WHEN SHOULD YOU HAVE BOLD, INCLUSIVE CONVERSATIONS?

Obviously it is important to minimize what may be perceived as an impact on productivity. All of the in-person sessions that I have facilitated occurred after normal work hours. In one case the session was held from 5:30–7:30 pm with a light dinner provided. Another client chose 4:00–6:00 pm. Some of the virtual sessions were conducted during lunch times, such as 11:30–1:00, and marketed as "lunch and learns," while others were convened during early morning time slots, such as 8:00–9:30 am.

Another *when* issue relates to on-time starts. A number of sessions, both in person and virtual, have not started on time as a result of participants arriving late. You will want to consider how much after the start time is acceptable. It can be disruptive if participants arrive too much after the start time. I would suggest stating in the invitation that no one will be admitted after (state time).

Preparing for One-One Conversations

This chapter focuses on planning for some type of group conversation. If the bold, inclusive conversation is going to be with just you and one other person, most of the advice still holds with a few caveats on how and when and where. I would recommend that one-one conversations of this nature not be conducted virtually, at least not if it is the first conversation. It is important to establish a connection that would be difficult to do in a virtual setting. If meeting in person is not possible, acknowledge the limitations of the technology up front and try to find a way to meet in person soon after this initial session. In terms of *when* to schedule the conversation, it may not be wise to hold a one-one session after normal working hours. It may send a message that this is not important or that the person is not important.

Consider this true example of an employee who became very anxious when it was time for her performance evaluation. Her palms got sweaty and she barely heard what her manager was saying because she was so nervous. The next year, rather than conduct the performance review in an office setting with the desk between them, the manager invited the employee for coffee. As they were walking to the company cafeteria, they chatted. When they sat down, the manager changed the subject and started to talk about a non-work topic. When the employee asked about her performance review, the manager responded, "We had it on the way to the cafeteria."

Changing the venue significantly reduced the employee's anxiety level. When it comes to discussing polarizing topics, *where* matters. A formal office setting with a desk in between the two parties can establish a power dynamic that hinders open dialogue. More informal, casual, neutral settings might break down physical and emotional barriers, enhance openness, and support a feeling of equity.

Avoid Spontaneous, Unplanned Conversations

The advice in this chapter focuses on how to prepare for bold, inclusive conversations. Sometimes you may find yourself in a situation where a difficult topic comes up spontaneously and you have not prepared for it. Perhaps, a polarizing topic such as race, religion, or politics just comes up in a meeting, or you are in the break room and you overhear a negative comment about your identity group, or somebody asks you a question about your stance on something political and you are taken by surprise. What should you do then? There is no way to prepare. It depends on a number of factors:

◆ Your relationship (How well do you know each other?)

◆ Your relative status (Are you coworkers, or is one of you a manager of the other?)

◆ Whether you have had bold conversations with this person (or these individuals) before

◆ Time constraints (Is there enough time to adequately address the topic?)

◆ Your emotional state and the emotional state of the other person/people

Nine times out of ten, you will want to discourage spontaneous conversation on these difficult topics. You might say, "That is an interesting question/perspective/comment, and to fully address it, I need some time to think about it. Can we table this and talk about it when we have more time to fully address it?" If the response is, "No, I would like to talk about it now," continue to push back. ("I understand that this is an important discussion. I want to be prepared. I hope that you can understand that. Let's schedule a time to delve into this in more detail.")

CHAPTER 4 ◆ TIPS FOR TALKING ABOUT IT!

◆ **Remember that preparation is different from readiness. Readiness is the longer-term process of introspection and learning more about those who are different from you (outlined in Chapters 2 and 3). Preparation is getting ready for an impending bold, inclusive conversation.**

◆ **In preparing for conversations, consider the why, who, what, how, where, and when.**

◆ **Keep in mind that the why, who, and what may unfold as the conversation process develops.**

- ◆ Recognize that virtual sessions can be as effective as in-person sessions depending on the why, who, and what; but in-person sessions may be more effective for one-one bold, inclusive conversations.

- ◆ In general, avoid spontaneous conversations on polarizing topics.

◆ ◆ ◆

Let the Conversations Begin: Search for Shared Meaning

*Most people do not listen with the intent to
understand; they listen with the intent to reply.*

STEPHEN R. COVEY, *The 7 Habits of Highly Effective People:
Powerful Lessons in Personal Change*

Now that you have a better understanding of the prerequisites for having bold, inclusive conversations and you have assessed your readiness, let's turn our attention to the actual conversation.

Remember this is a process and not a singular event. (See the figure on the next page, which is Figure 1 from the preface, repeated here for your convenience.) There may need to be several conversations that build on one another to reach the desired outcome of shared meaning and ultimately the ability to deeply understand each other's perspectives, which we explore in Chapter 6. If you and the other(s) engaging in the conversation already have experience, perhaps one conversation will suffice, depending on the topic and the desired outcomes. This chapter primarily addresses those with limited skills to have bold, inclusive conversations, and therefore, the assumption is that multiple conversations will be necessary. Use your judgment as to how many conversations may be needed in your situation.

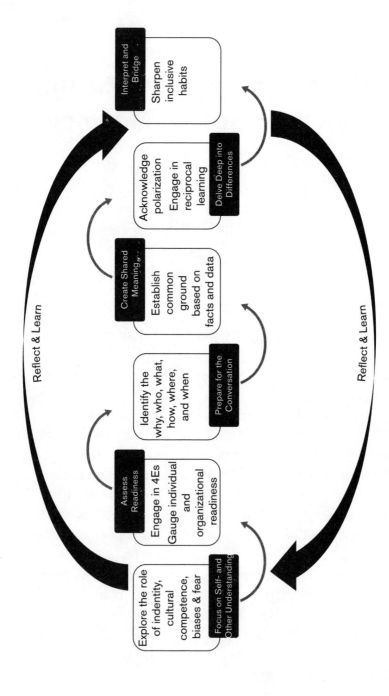

A MODEL FOR BOLD, INCLUSIVE CONVERSATIONS

GUIDANCE FOR THE FIRST CONVERSATION

Let's look at the following scenario and work through the process at a high level for what might happen at the first meeting.

Jake is a white manager. Rodney, an African American, reports to Jake. Rodney has come to Jake to ask why the company has not taken a visible position on the recent killings of African American men. Rodney shares that these situations have left him anxious and fearful, and he has overheard other white employees be dismissive about these incidents. Rodney asks for Jake's advice. He suggests that maybe the team should get together to talk about it.

Note: While this example is about race because I feel that race is one of the most difficult topics, you can substitute other polarizing subjects and use this same process.

As the Manager, What Should You Do?

Suggest a one-one meeting at another mutually convenient time with Rodney before agreeing to convene a group session. Do not attempt the conversation without the readiness and preparation outlined in the previous chapters.

At this juncture, many managers will feel anxious and may want to bring in someone from Human Resources or the Legal Department to be a part of the initial discussion. *Please* resist that temptation as the *first* thing you would do. Often when the topic is about some group that is protected by law (e.g., race, gender, age, sexual orientation, disability), the immediate concern is the legal vulnerability, and many managers have been taught to mitigate risks by consulting with HR or Legal. HR and Legal are invaluable resources to the organization. However, sometimes managers would rather hand over these types of issues to one of these departments, abdicating their role. I am suggesting that, as the first step, managers should gather more information before engaging any other stakeholders.

Rodney may feel even more vulnerable and marginalized if others are involved before he has an opportunity to state his case. He may not see this as a legal issue at all. Rodney may simply want to have a candid conversation with Jake to talk about a topic that is of concern. Bringing in legal counsel or someone from HR could diminish the possibility of establishing a trusting relationship, as Rodney may feel that Jake thinks he may be contemplating a legal action against the company, which in turn can shut down the possibility of conversation altogether. He may think that Jake considers him a legal risk just because he's black. You can well imagine that this can negatively impact trust.

I know of an organization that faced a similar situation. An African American HR manager met with the white Senior Vice-President of HR to share that African American employees in her division of the company did not feel that they were being treated with the same respect as their white counterparts. They did not feel included. The African American HR manager simply wanted to discuss the concerns with her boss. However, on the advice of their internal legal department, the company immediately decided to hire an external law firm to conduct a full investigation of the situation without further discussion or consultation with the HR manager who brought the concerns to leadership. This left the African American HR manager feeling frustrated, ignored, and excluded.

While the HR manager did not think that it was necessary to involve legal counsel, company policy may have dictated that Legal be consulted on matters relating to race, gender, and other groups that are protected by law. In the situation above in which Rodney wants to discuss the situation with Jake, Rodney may ask Jake not to involve others at this juncture.

Possible language for Rodney might be "I realize that given the nature of my concern and that we don't typically discuss these topics at work, it may be company policy to engage HR and/or Legal. Is it possible for just the two of us to have a conversation first and then you can let me know if you feel you need to go outside the department?"

As the manager, Jake should learn as much as he can about all perspectives on the topic before the scheduled time for the conversation. Jake may want to consult HR for guidance but not have a representative present at this initial meeting. Before meeting with Rodney, Jake should prepare by doing the following:

- Explore his own perspectives and question why he feels as he does about the issue.

- Learn about the topic from other perspectives.

- Assess how much trust there is with Rodney by considering previous situations that may have either built or eroded trust.

- Establish that the purpose of the meeting is for him to just listen to Rodney.

- Consider his own conflict resolution style as discussed in Chapter 3. Is it engagement, discussion, accommodation, or dynamic? Consider Rodney's conflict resolution style.

Rodney should also prepare. Before meeting with Jake, he should do the following:

- Learn as much as he can about all perspectives on the situation for his own understanding.

- Explore his own perspectives and question why he feels as he does.

- Learn as much as he can about the topic from the perspectives of others.

- Assess how much trust there is with Jake by considering previous situations that may have built or eroded trust.

- Ask himself if he believes that Jake as a white man could not possibly understand how he feels, and if so, what evidence there is of this. Consider how he will effectively engage in the conversation if he feels this way. Plan to share information that might enhance Jake's understanding.

- Consider his conflict resolution style as discussed in Chapter 3. Is it engagement, discussion, accommodation, or dynamic? Consider Jake's conflict resolution style.

CONVERSATION 1:
JAKE LISTENS TO RODNEY

The recommendations outlined for this conversation assume that both Rodney and Jake are new at having bold conversations. See Chapter 6 for a guide for assessing where to start the conversation.

Considering Rodney initiated the conversation, Jake's role should be just to listen, not to interject his opinion or to debate. The specific goals of the first meeting might include the following:

Create a "Brave Zone." A brave zone encompasses a safe zone but goes further because it gives you permission to be courageous in saying things that might be uncomfortable.

Agree on Confidentiality Parameters. Jake might say something like: "This conversation is just between us at this point. If I feel that I have to escalate your concerns, I will let you know first and we can talk about the best way to move forward."

Enhance Jake's Understanding. These topics are very personal and are often at the core of one's identity. As highlighted in Chapter 3, you don't understand if you have not had the employee's experience. Therefore Jake should refrain from saying "I understand how you feel." Rather say something like: "I want to better understand how you may be feeling and how this is impacting you at work."

Rodney Shares His Perspective. Rodney should not expect Jake to have solutions at this juncture or even understand all of his perspective. Rodney should assume positive intent and make sure his presentation is balanced between his perspective and the facts as he knows them. He should not point blame or be judgmental. He should try to present in as neutral a way as possible and avoid saying things like, "I don't think most white people understand." How could Rodney really know what most white people think? Instead, he should say something like, "I know that it is sometimes hard for me to understand issues that may not impact me directly." (Rodney is using an "I" statement, which will not put Jake on the defensive.)

Recognize Cultural Differences. Rodney's culture may be more or less emotionally expressive than Jake's. For certain cultures, too much emotional display is off-putting. For other cultures too little emotional display suggests you don't care, as discussed in Chapter 3. Rodney should find the balance that will work while still being authentic. It will be important for Rodney to use "I" language and not to project his feelings on others. For example, do not say: "I think I speak for all African Americans on the team." Rodney can only speak for himself.

Rodney might present some of the following facts:

- One in four African American males is likely to do prison time in his lifetime.[1]
- Although 31.8 percent of the people shot by police are black, black people account for only 13.5 percent of the population.[2]
- According to the US Bureau of Justice Statistics (BJS) in 2013, non-Hispanic black males accounted for 37 percent of the total male prison population, even though they make up only 6.5 percent of the population.[3]

Next, Rodney may share his personal experience:

- I realize that the reasons for these statistics are complex including unconscious bias, poverty, education, historical exclusion (e.g., job discrimination, redlining), violence in many urban black communities.
- I have personally been stopped by police despite not breaking the law. In the black community it is known as driving while black.
- Every time I hear of another shooting, I become more fearful, not only for myself but also for my son.

The facts are critical, but as stated earlier, understanding individual experiences is also key.

Listen: Jake's role during this conversation is to simply listen. I think there is universal agreement that the key to effective dialogue is listening. Listening to understand when the topics are polarizing requires more intentionality. Most experts posit that we listen to defend or reply rather than listen to understand. It is really important to listen only for understanding, especially during the first session.

How do you **listen for understanding?**

◆ When you find yourself disagreeing, stop and ask yourself why. Commit to yourself that you will explore your contrary opinion later during the reflection phase (outlined later in this chapter) and quickly get back to listening.

◆ Make a mental note of those things that you don't understand. It is better not to take notes. However if you really feel that you have to as a reminder to yourself, make sure you ask for permission to take notes and to let the employee know that the purpose is for your own research and follow-up.

◆ Historically marginalized groups may have a hard time believing that someone from the dominant group has positive intent. There may be huge trust issues that make meaningful conversation more difficult. Jake can demonstrate positive intent with body language that demonstrates that he is engaged. This might include but not necessarily be limited to eye contact, good posture, affirming nods, neutral expressions, and clarifying questions.

◆ Ask only clarifying questions. "Could you tell me more about that? I did not understand your last point. Could you elaborate?"

These techniques will provide evidence that you are really listening for understanding.

Expect non-closure at the first conversation: You actually want non-closure at this juncture. It is simply a conversation where Jake will practice intense listening and Rodney will practice sharing from his perspective. The conversation might end with Jake saying something like "Thank you for sharing your perspective, Rodney. I really learned a lot and now would like some time to reflect on what you said and perhaps do some more learning. Can we agree to meet again in two weeks?" Jake should leave enough time to do his homework but not so much that Rodney feels ignored.

Rodney should be prepared to recommend resources to support Jake in gaining greater knowledge about the issues facing African Americans in the criminal justice system, such as the books *The People's History of the United States*,[4] *History of White People*,[5] *Justice in America: The Separate Realities of Blacks and Whites*,[6] and *The New Jim Crow: Mass Incarceration in the Age of Colorblindness*;[7] and the 2016 Netflix documentary *13th*,[8] which examines the US criminal justice system with a historical and racial lens. This will support Jake in better understanding the contextual implications for the facts that Rodney has shared, as discussed earlier

Following the First Conversation: Reflect and Learn

It will be important for both Jake and Rodney to reflect on the outcome of the first conversation before moving forward.

Jake should ask himself:

- How did I feel about the conversation?
- What did I learn?
- What did I disagree with and why?
- What surprised me and why?
- What else do I need to learn about before I have the next conversation?

Rodney should ask himself:

- How did I feel about the conversation?

- Was Jake really listening? What were the clues that he was/was not listening?
- Was my presentation clear, concise, and cohesive?
- How did my natural engagement style of communication show up? Was I able to balance my emotional expressiveness, knowing that Jake is more discussion style?
- Did I just talk about my opinion, or was I balanced with my perspective and facts as I know them?
- Are there points of clarification that I need to get more information about? What else do I need to learn before the next conversation?

They might also want to seek advice from a colleague or friend who may be more skilled at understanding these issues.

CONVERSATION 2:
SEARCHING FOR SHARED MEANING

The second conversation has two objectives: (1) for Jake to share what he has learned and ask more questions as may be needed; (2) to search for shared understanding. Rodney's role during the first part of the second conversation is primarily to listen to Jake, using all of the listening guidelines outlined above, and answer the questions posed in the last conversation and during the reflection and learning period. During the second part of this conversation, the goal is to try to find common ground—to get to a place of shared meaning.

Conversation 2, Phase 1:
Jake Shares, Rodney Listens

Jake should ask questions to clarify Rodney's perspective as a result of his additional knowledge garnered during the reflection and learning period. Jake might say, "I really appreciated our last meeting. I have had time to reflect and learn more. I have some additional questions, if you don't mind. I admit that I am new to understanding the complexities of race. I do want to learn more, so I hope you will bear with me if you think some of my questions are naïve or uninformed or just plain stupid."

Rodney might say, "I think I sometimes expect others to know more about the issues of my culture than they do, and I also sometimes resent having to be the teacher. This is something I am working on, so if I seem impatient or assume that you should already know something, I ask that you are patient with me."

Jake could respond, "Great—we can be patient with each other."

This type of exchange helps to build a common ground and also trust. Each party is admitting the need to learn something (i.e., they have something in common). They are willing to be vulnerable in this regard, which helps to build trust.

Cut Each Other Some Slack

I often hear from employees from historically marginalized groups that they are tired of educating whites about the issues that they face. The sentiment goes something like this: "After all of these years of racial strife in this county, white people should get it. I am tired of trying to teach white people what it is like."

My answer goes something like this: "From your perspective, maybe more white people should understand your worldview, but not everyone does; nor will everyone ever totally understand. Maybe they have not been exposed or had experiences or education (the 4Es outlined in Chapter 3) to be able to understand your worldview from your perspective. Maybe they have not walked in your shoes."

I recommend that we cut each other some slack, increase our patience quotient, and take advantage of teachable moments. I ask the historically marginalized groups, "If not you, then who will teach them?" Rodney should patiently answer questions, even if they seem basic, naïve, or common knowledge. He should try not to show an emotional response or tone in his voice that would suggest he thinks that Jake is asking a stupid or common-knowledge question. A judgmental reaction will likely shut down open dialogue.

Recognize that we don't know what we don't know.

It is important to note that Rodney's capacity to be patient and understanding of Jake's inexperience will depend on Rodney's current emotional state. Again, these topics can be emotionally draining, and that is okay. It is critical that Rodney assess his own state of being able to engage patiently and productively. At this point, he should take the self-assessment on the next page.

Conversation 2, Phase 2:
Getting to Shared Meaning

The conversation should now transition to getting to shared understanding. The **Ladder of Inference**, as shown in Figure 5, is a helpful model in understanding the complexities associated with trying to find common ground.[9]

We need to recognize that while the same pool of data may be available to everyone, we may select data on the basis of our identity group, our worldview, and what is important to us. We therefore draw interpretations based on our assumptions about what is true or not.

These assumptions and interpretations (conclusions) lead us to actions based on our beliefs. The DNA model highlighted in Chapter 2 can be useful at this stage of the dialogue.

ARE YOU READY TO GET TO SHARED MEANING?
(A self-assessment)

- What am I feeling right now and why?
- Why did this event induce this particular reaction?
- Am I able to see the situation from all sides or am I looking at it in a polarized way?
- Do I realize that these situations are complex and not necessarily easily resolved?
- Am I expecting too much from my coworkers, colleagues, and friends?
- Do I have a trusted adviser/friend/confidant with whom I can be open and authentic?
- Am I fixed in my opinions or am I willing to learn how it might feel from the perspective of the other?
- What energy do I have to expend to learn more about the situation from the perspective of the other?
- Am I willing to put in the time that it will take?
- Am I willing to admit that I have biases and blind spots that may be getting in the way of my judgments?
- Am I willing to cut my coworkers some slack if they don't seem to understand?
- Can I live with the fact that some people really just may not care the way I do?
- Can I live with the fact that I may not be able to make them care?
- Am I willing to be patient and recognize that it may take some time and many teachable moments for my coworkers to understand my perspective?
- Am I prepared for, and comfortable with, agreeing to disagree?

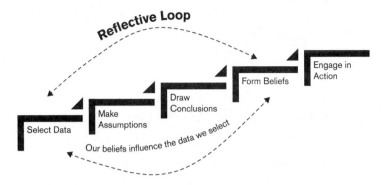

FIGURE 5. LADDER OF INFERENCE

Adapted from *The Fifth Discipline Fieldbook,* by Peter M. Senge,
Art Kleiner, Charlotte Roberts, Richard B. Ross, and Bryan J. Smith.

◆ Describe the behavior.

◆ Navigate your understanding by exploring different
interpretations. What are your feelings about each
interpretation?

◆ Adapt your actions based on your interpretation.

Let's apply the DNA model to one of the issues Rodney
raised. One of the behaviors Rodney describes is the rising number of unarmed black men who have been killed
by police. Possible interpretations include (1) black men are
more likely to be criminals, (2) racism leads to this outcome,
and (3) racial disproportionality in the criminal justice system is based on a complex web of socio-economic, historic,
and race-based reasons.

If Jake believes interpretation #1, he would have little
empathy and the polarization would continue. If Jake or
Rodney believe interpretation #2 only, polarization is also
likely to continue. (Remember the danger of a single story,
discussed in Chapter 2.) Interpretation #3 is a much broader

perspective, which allows Jake and Rodney to continue to dig deeper and expand their mutual understanding.

Here is how a shared-meaning dialogue might start.

JAKE: Based on what we have talked about these last two meetings, where do you think we are? I would like to think that we have created some shared understanding of the situation.

RODNEY: I think we have to some degree.

JAKE: Let's see if we can identify those areas of agreement and where we still have some opportunities.

RODNEY: Sounds good.

Some potential areas of agreement for Jake and Rodney:

- We all want to be safe.
- We all want to be able to trust those in charge of keeping us safe.
- Historically, African Americans have had very different experiences than white people, and there is a need to foster deeper understanding of these differences.
- African Americans have unspoken concerns about the killing of unarmed black men.
- These types of stresses can impact engagement and productivity.
- We don't know what we don't know, and we all have a lot to learn about each other to have effective dialogue.

At this juncture, these agreements are fairly noncontroversial. Even though Jake and Rodney have reached some level of agreement, there may still be different interpretations (e.g., how safety is interpreted by Jake may be very different from how Rodney interprets the concept of safety). For example, Jake may have never thought about or have to think about being safe on the Metro track, as the gay, Muslim, Middle Eastern employee mentioned in Chapter 1 believes he does. In other words, Jake may not interpret safety as being correlated with his identity as a white male.

Reflect and Learn More

We do not learn from experience . . . we
learn from reflecting on experience.
John Dewey[10]

After each conversation, there must be a reflection period before the next encounter. At this juncture, each party has had an opportunity to be heard. You must assess whether more listening is needed to achieve shared meaning or if you can venture deeper in discussing your differences.

Integrate Bold, Inclusive Conversations into Existing Processes

The process of getting to shared meaning should not be taken lightly. It may take several conversations and opportunities to learn and reflect to attain this goal. Please note that there are no set number of conversations to get to this point. It could take one or ten, for that matter. It depends on a number of different factors such as the topic, openness to accept each other's perspective, the amount of new information that needs processing and understanding, and so on. You will have to learn to be comfortable with non-closure. You may never get to closure because this is a process—a journey and not a destination.

You might be thinking, *We have a business to run. We really don't have time for all of these side conversations that have nothing to do with our real work.*

Consider allocating some time for additional conversations as a part of a weekly one-one or team session that is already a part of your normal business processes. For example, if you typically have a one-hour one-one for work updates, incorporate the continued conversation as a part of that time. If you have a cross-cultural learning program, as discussed in Chapter 3, or reciprocal mentoring, make it a part of that process. In other words, try to incorporate bold, inclusive conversations into existing structures.

Let's assume that Rodney and Jake have achieved enough shared meaning that they are now ready for the next conversation, which will focus on their differences. The guidance for delving into differences is explored in Chapter 6.

CHAPTER 5 ◆ TIPS FOR TALKING ABOUT IT!

◆ Plan to have several conversations that build on one another to reach the desired outcome of shared meaning and the ability to deeply understand each other's perspectives.

◆ Remember: bold, inclusive conversations are processes, not events.

◆ Foster your ability to listen; it is the most important skill during the initial conversation.

◆ Schedule and plan for the conversation. Avoid spontaneous dialogue.

◆ If you are the initiator of the conversation, be prepared to state your case based on the facts and your perspective.

◆ If you are not the initiator of the conversation, be prepared to just listen, and only ask questions for clarification.

◆ Plan to reflect and engage in additional learning before the next conversation.

◆ If you were primarily listening during the first conversation, be prepared to share your perspective and ask questions during the second conversation.

◆ If you were the original convener, prepare to listen during the second conversation. Be patient with potential mistakes and misinformation. Be prepared to clarify points without judgment.

◆ Strive for shared meaning during the second conversation. Utilize the Ladder of Inference and the DNA Model to reach mutual understanding.

◆ Keep in mind that there is no set number of conversations that will get you to shared meaning. It could be one or ten.

◆ Integrate bold, inclusive conversations as a part of your normal one-one or team discussions.

SIX

◆ ◆ ◆

Let the Conversations Continue: Interpret and Bridge Differences

There is no greater agony than bearing
an untold story inside you.

MAYA ANGELOU, *I Know Why the Caged Bird Sings*[1]

Jake and Rodney are now ready to delve into their different perspectives. This is their third conversation. Readiness to delve into differences may happen by the third conversation or it may not. It could happen before then, depending on the readiness and preparation of each party, as shown in our model for Bold, Inclusive Conversations. (See the figure on page 88.)

It is hard to say how you will know when you are ready. It will be a feeling of greater mutual understanding. You will feel that you have amassed sufficient information about the other person or cultural group. You will sense that you are at a different place—a shift has occurred—and your worldview is different from when you started the first conversation. The table on the next page is a guide for determining when you might be ready for deeper conversations around polarizing topics.

ACKNOWLEDGE THE ELEPHANT IN THE ROOM

Delving into the differences is the most difficult part of the conversation process. Acknowledging that polarized opinions exist is the first step.

AM I READY? A GUIDE

Readiness Level	New at This (have not had bold, inclusive conversations)	Some Experience (have had a few conversations)	Very Experienced
Get Ready	Focus mostly on self-understanding and other understanding. (Chapters 2–3).	Focus mostly on other under-standing (Chapter 3). This level assumes you have experience with at least one or two cultures other than your own.	Focus mostly on exploring differences.
Prepare	Make sure you are prepared (Chapter 4).	Reflect on lessons learned from previous sessions. What would you do differently?	Reflect on lessons learned from previous sessions. What would you do differently?
Converse	Listen, learn, clarify, and reflect. Be patient. Build trust.	Listen, learn, and reflect. Question, clarify, and share your perspective. Be patient. Build trust.	Listen, learn, and reflect. Question, clarify, and share your perspective. Share deep personal stories. Be vulnerable. Share points of disagreement. Discuss ways to bridge differences to achieve a win-win. Trust level should already be high.
Primary Goal	Listen in order to come to shared meaning.	Deeply explore differences.	Bridge cultural differences. Strive for reciprocal empathy.

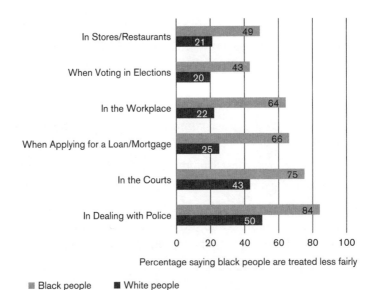

FIGURE 6. DIFFERENCES IN PERCEPTIONS
OF HOW BLACK PEOPLE ARE TREATED IN THE UNITED STATES
Adapted from Pew, 2016

Continuing with our example of Rodney and Jake, let's look at the polarization that they might acknowledge at this juncture.

In Chapter 1, I highlighted the study that only 44 percent of white people were very concerned about the killing of Philando Castile and Alton Sterling (two black men), compared to 77 percent of black people. However, this is not the only topic for which black and white people are polarized.

A 2016 Pew study highlighted in Figure 6 shows the division in perceptions on a number of different issues, including on how black people are treated by the criminal justice system, in housing, in the workplace, in stores, in restaurants, and when voting.[2] These conflicting views obviously make it more difficult to have bold, courageous conversations. Before progress can be made, that polarization must be revealed. Acknowledge the elephant in the room, and admit that polarization exists.

The reflection and learning that Jake and Rodney have engaged in up to this point should have already surfaced some of the reasons for polarization on these issues. So both Jake and Rodney should be armed with more knowledge. That does not necessarily mean that there has been a total shift so that they each completely agree with the other's perspective.

Remember in the last chapter, they were able to come to some shared meaning, mostly on the less controversial facts. Jake may still have a hard time believing that the police actually profile a certain race for no legitimate reason, and Rodney may still believe that Jake's white privilege keeps him from seeing the full picture.

Continuing with Jake and Rodney's conversations from Chapter 5, the third conversation might start with something like this.

JAKE: I have been reading a lot of the issue of how black people are treated in the criminal justice system. I really had no idea of the disparities. It looks like the reasons are fairly complex.

RODNEY: They are. Do you agree that it is largely due to discrimination?

JAKE: I am not sure. I always thought that our justice system was pretty color blind. If you do the crime, you pay your time, so to speak.

RODNEY: (Rephrasing rather than defending at this point) So what I hear you saying is that you think the system is fair.

JAKE: Yes, for the most part, I think so, or at least I thought so. The stats do show that blacks commit more crimes than whites.

DISTINGUISH DIFFERENT INTERPRETATIONS
AND CLARIFY DEFINITIONS

Let's consider the interpretation of fairness. Fairness to Jake might look like the rules are applied the same to everybody regardless of race (the minimization worldview described in Chapter 2). He may envision a meritocracy.

For Rodney, fairness may be less fixed and depend on circumstances. Rodney might think that it is fairer to consider context and history in making the decision and not necessarily treat everyone the same.

For example, if someone steals food because they have no money, because they cannot find employment, because they have been discriminated against, should their punishment be the same as someone who has money and a good job but steals food? Jake and Rodney will need to explore ethical considerations such as this and use the reflect-and-learn cycle for further exploration.

To have meaningful conversations about difference, we should define and clarify terms. If there are different interpretations, keep them all visible (perhaps on a flip chart or captured on projection device). At this juncture, do not debate the validity of the different definitions; simply acknowledge and make note of them.

UNCOVER YOUR DIFFERENT PERSPECTIVES

When we start a conversation from a polarization mindset, we typically have a very simplistic understanding of the topic or situation. However, if we have gone through the steps of learning more about all aspects—broadening our knowledge and reflecting—we are better prepared to have an informed opinion, to be curious about the other's opinion, and to listen with an open mind. We are at that point operating at acceptance on the Intercultural Development Continuum discussed in Chapter 2.

At this juncture, the conversation may go something like this.

JAKE: While I am disturbed by the disproportionality in the statistics showing the number of incarcerated blacks, the facts also show that blacks perpetuate more violent crimes, overall, and much of it is black-on-black crime, is it not?

RODNEY: Black-on-black crime is concerning, but you have to consider that even though the ratio of black homicides against black victims is greater, the number of white murderers far exceeds the number of black murderers.

JAKE: Well yes, I would expect the numbers to be bigger because there are more whites in the population than blacks. Isn't the ratio the problem?

RODNEY: Yes, it is certainly a problem, but why do you think black men are incarcerated at six times their numbers in the population? That is a ratio too. Do you think that black men are more prone to be criminals?

JAKE: I don't know about "prone to be criminals," but the facts would suggest that they are. However, what I have learned through this process is that the reasons for these statistics are extremely complex and I need to keep learning more. I just think it is sad when anybody is murdered senselessly, and I don't understand why black people would want to kill other black people. I also realize now though, why, as an African American male, you might be more fearful about your safety. I did not understand that before.

RODNEY: Part of the reason for black-on-black crime is the feeling of worthlessness and helplessness on the part of many young black men. The statistics clearly show different outcomes for black males as early as pre-school. They are stereotyped as less intelligent and more aggressive, and, in some cases, this becomes a self-fulfilling prophecy.

JAKE: It did not happen to you. Look at how great you turned out. I really think life is what we make it in the end. People can make lemonade out of lemons, you know. There are a lot of stories about you people who have overcome the odds. I don't understand why more of you people don't.

At this juncture, Rodney became frustrated and somewhat angry. He nearly lost it when Jake said "you people." Jake probably did not know why those two words were such a hot button for Rodney. (See Chapter 7.) Remembering his emotional intelligence skills, Rodney knew he needed to manage his emotions at that point. He did not want to show Jake how frustrated he had become. He and Jake seem to be at an impasse. Rather than continue the conversation, it is time to pause.

RODNEY: (In a neutral tone) No it did not happen to me. Every person's circumstance is different. I think we have gone far enough for this conversation. I would like to refer you to some additional information on this topic that might help. I would also like to suggest that during our next conversation we talk about our respective life experiences. I do want you to know more about who I am, my experiences, and I would like to know the same about you.

JAKE: Yes, I would like that, too. Let's plan on it.

KNOW WHEN TO PUT THE
CONVERSATION ON PAUSE

Rodney and Jake have come to an impasse. They should stop, agree to do some more reflection and learning, and come back at another time to continue. When there is a deadlock around ideologies, emotions may run high and both parties might sink back into polarization. Continue to frame these conversations as skill development. Remember that when learning a skill, there may be times you just can't grasp a particular point, so you leave it for some period and come back to it with fresh eyes and ears.

Tell Your Story

Storytellers, by the very act of telling, communicate a radical learning that changes lives and the world: telling stories is a universally accessible means through which people make meaning.

Chris Cavanaugh, Olympic swimmer[3]

When Jake and Rodney come back together for their fourth conversation, they have agreed to tell their stories. Storytelling is a very powerful learning tool. Everybody has a diversity story, regardless of their race, gender, and sexual orientation. However, we have to be ready to hear someone else's story in a way that will have a compelling impact and foster greater understanding.

Telling one's story when the parties are still polarized can move them deeper into polarization, because at this stage, they are still wedded totally to their own opinions and may consider the story an excuse, an exaggeration, not relevant to the facts, not the norm; or they may use any other similar rationale that would deny the validity of the story.

Conversely, it could have a positive outcome—an epiphany that moves individuals out of polarization to a place of greater understanding. I have seen it work both ways. In one situation, after a compelling story from an African American woman about being labeled as an angry black woman, one of her white female colleagues, said, "I don't think that has anything to do with race at all. I could say the same label happens for white women." It effectively invalidated the African American woman's story.

On the other hand, the story of the gay, Muslim male who was afraid to stand close to the edge of the Metro platform, referenced earlier in the book, provided an aha experience for one of the white senior leaders, who was shocked that anyone would be carrying such a fear with them every day. He had told his story during the third conversation with the employee affinity groups.

Rodney and Jake have not yet shared their deep personal stories. They have pretty much stayed in the head (facts and logic). Assuming that Jake is more discussion style, it was appropriate to provide a more logical, fact-based argument, as opposed to a more emotional delivery that personal stories may generate. It may now be the right time for them to have a conversation about their life experiences and how these experiences have shaped who they are.

There are pros and cons to placing this type of sharing at this point in the process, rather than during the first two conversations structured around listening. The advantage of telling one's story early on is that it fosters openness and transparency, which can build trust and empathy, and, as mentioned above, it may lead to a transformative aha moment early on that can get one to delve into differences sooner. The drawback is there may not be enough mutual trust that early in the process so that the parties feel comfortable sharing at this deep level. One of the primary purposes of the first three conversations is to build trust. However, as stated above, it could deepen the polarization because of the lack of foundational knowledge at that early juncture.

If there is adequate readiness early in the process based on the self-assessment in Chapter 3, sharing one's story can be quite impactful during the listening phase.

Where Do Jake and Rodney Go from Here?

So what's next for Jake and Rodney after they share their respective stories in the fourth conversation? They need to keep chipping away at more mutual understanding, which does not necessarily mean agreement or consensus. Perhaps they incorporate further conversations into their regular one-one meetings as recommended in Chapter 5. There may come a point where they agree to disagree while still respecting each other's right to have a different point of view.

Rodney and Jake now both have a greater capacity to have bold, inclusive conversations. They have done the hard readiness work recommended in Chapters 2 and 3 and have had some breakthrough conversations that shifted perspectives. The level of trust is enhanced so that if there is another polarizing topic that they want to discuss, they are not starting from scratch. They may need to repeat some of the readiness steps to learn about a new topic but will be able to get to delving into their differences much faster.

Rodney had initially requested that there be a team meeting to discuss his concerns about the killing of unarmed black men. Jake is in a much better position now to make a decision about the advisability of such a session. He knows the process that he needed to go through to get to this point. Rodney, too, has a better vantage point. They decided that Jake would share what he had learned at a team meeting, stressing the importance of supporting each other during times of stress and trauma. This would be an opportunity for the team to listen to Jake as the leader and for Jake to answer questions other employees might have. Depending on the interest and readiness of the team, Jake would decide if additional conversations were warranted. In addition, Rodney would seek support from the black employee network group as an opportunity to commiserate with others who may share his fears and anxieties.

The End Point: Reciprocal Empathy

If there *is* an end-point to bold, inclusive conversations—and I contend that there really isn't because it is a journey not a destination—it is reciprocal empathy. If we can get to the point of reciprocal empathy (i.e., the ability to know what it is like to be the "other"), we increase the likelihood of generating new ways to engage with each other.

When we engage with each other, we have the opportunity to learn more about each other's similarities and differences, build better relationships, and improve trust. In the workplace, employees will feel more valued, respected, and more motivated to give their all. This, in turn, leads to greater productivity, engagement, and innovation. One of the participants from a dialogue session noted in Chapter 1 summed it up this way: "I will go back to work now knowing that others are feeling like I do. Just being able to openly talk about it makes me feel better, and I can go back to giving my all. Somebody understands."

Celebrate Little Breakthroughs and Keep Practicing

I keep reiterating that this is a process, one that has no specific ending. Learning how to have bold, inclusive conversations is a journey, not a destination. You have to keep chipping away at it a little bit at a time, just like any other competency. If you are learning to play the piano, you keep practicing until you are able to play more difficult pieces. There may come a time when you don't have to practice as much because you have mastered the skill. However, to keep your skills fresh, you will always need to practice some. Hopefully there will not be a need to have regular conversations about polarizing topics, but you want to be ready when the need arises.

There will be little gains and some big gains along the way. Celebrate them all.

CHAPTER 6 ◆ TIPS FOR TALKING ABOUT IT!

◆ Recognize that it is hard to predict when you will be ready to delve into deep, polarizing differences. First, you will feel some type of shift in your worldview perspective.

◆ Acknowledge the points of polarization at the beginning of the conversation in order to delve deeply into the topic.

◆ Clarify meanings and interpretations. Allow for multiple interpretations as you sort out your different perspectives.

◆ When you reach an impasse, put the conversation on pause.

◆ Learn to manage your emotions when there is disagreement.

◆ Build trust before sharing your story, so that it will be understood and validated.

◆ Recognize that there is no real end point to bold, inclusive conversations. It is a journey, not a destination. You keep developing and learning.

◆ Seek reciprocal empathy.

◆ Celebrate the little breakthroughs as much as the big wins.

SEVEN

◆ ◆ ◆

Sharpen Inclusive Habits

Inclusion starts with I and takes all of us.

MARY-FRANCES WINTERS

The need to have bold, inclusive conversations on polarizing topics in the workplace will ebb and flow. Polarizing topics will not always be front and center, and there may be some subjects, such as politics, that you will want to continue to discourage. However, when politics or other polarizing topics come up, you want to be ready and prepared so that the outcome has a positive impact on the work climate. This final chapter provides guidance for honing inclusive habits that you will want to practice on a regular basis—even if it is not about a polarizing topic—and some language to be aware of that can encumber inclusion.

INCLUSIVE HABITS TO LIVE BY

I have found that these habits can enhance our capacity for inclusion.

Acknowledging: You don't know everything; there is always something to learn.

Legitimizing: Other perspectives are just as valid as yours and should be listened to for the purpose of understanding, not necessarily agreement.

Listening: Listen to understand. Listen for your own cultural assumptions, perceptions, and expectations.

Reflecting: Spend more time reflecting on your own values and beliefs. Why do you believe what you believe? Why would someone believe the opposite? Can you respect the beliefs of others even when you don't agree?

Describing: Learn to describe the behavior before providing your interpretation, and expand the number of interpretations you consider. Use the DNA tool outlined in Chapter 2 to support you in this habit.

Contextualizing: Consider the circumstances, conditions, and history of the topic for which you are having a bold, inclusive conversation. Provide the proper context for the conversation.

Pausing: Always pause before you provide your opinion on a polarizing topic. Take a deep breath. Think about what you are going to say. Pause to be more patient as well. Be patient of mistakes. Be patient of the frustrations of historically marginalized groups. Be patient with people who don't understand your experience as a member of a historically marginalized group.

Accepting: Accepting does not mean agreeing. You are accepting that there are myriad worldviews, and it is important to learn more about them. Accepting is better than tolerating. How do you feel when someone tells you that they will tolerate you? Not so good, right? Many diversity programs advocate for tolerance. Work to move from tolerance to acceptance.

Questioning: Show genuine interest in others. Be curious, not judgmental, about their experiences.

Respecting: Respect the dignity of every person even when you don't agree with them. Separate the person from the position. Practice the Platinum Rule, by treating others the way they want to be treated.

Apologizing: What do you do when you make a mistake or say the wrong thing because you just did not know? As I suggest in Chapter 3, we have to learn to be patient of mistakes and cut each other some slack. If you say something that offends someone else, genuinely apologize. The impact on the other person may be very different from what you intended. Do not defend your comment. Simply say, "I am sorry. Please help me understand why that was offensive." Consider it a teaching moment. Refer to the next section in this chapter for guidance on triggers and micro-inequities that different groups might find offensive.

Connecting: Making meaningful connections across difference is one sure way of breaking down barriers and enhancing our capacity for empathy and shared understanding.

Empathizing: Sympathy leads to patronization and pity. Empathy allows you to see the situation from the perspective of the other person.

TRIGGERS AND MICRO-INEQUITIES: BARRIERS TO BOLD, INCLUSIVE CONVERSATIONS

There are some key triggers that we should avoid in our attempts to be inclusive—words and phrases that may be considered offensive, derogatory, or insensitive by different groups. These slights are sometimes referred to as **micro-inequities**, seemingly small, offhand comments that build up over time and erode trust and the possibility of meaningful conversations. Note: this is not an exhaustive list. I am providing some examples to help you as you prepare for your bold, inclusive conversations. It is also not an attempt at "political correctness." Rather, I want to provide an understanding of why certain terms may be offensive. I don't want you to try to memorize the list. Reflect on it to support you in advancing your cultural competence.

Some key triggers for **African Americans** include the following:

"You are so articulate." It suggests that the speaker is surprised and has a preconceived notion that black people are less intelligent than white people.

"You people." This perpetuates the "us-and-them" syndrome and suggests that the person addressed doesn't belong here. It also stereotypes by lumping all black people together, implying they are all alike.

References to monkeys/apes. Black people have been compared to monkeys throughout history in a way that implies they are less human. For example, Michelle Obama has been likened to apes and monkeys throughout her time as First Lady. Even the phrase "don't monkey around" can be a trigger.

"When I look at you, I don't see color." We have been taught that it is best to be color blind and just treat everybody the same. Color blindness negates the person of color's identity.

"American is a melting pot." Some people cannot melt because their difference is visible. A more appropriate metaphor might be a stew, a symphony, or a salad.

"There is only one race—the human race." This is a minimization statement and deemphasizes the unique culture and experiences of people of color.

"I am not a racist. I have several black friends." The speaker may not be a racist. However, the racial makeup of one's

group of friends does not determine whether or not one's attitudes and behaviors are prejudicial.

"I don't think that has/had anything to do with race." For a person of color, everything has something to do with race. The sheer fact of being visibly different makes it impossible to eliminate race from any interaction. If the person of color thinks that race plays a factor, then that perception is his or her truth. It is important to acknowledge, legitimize, and understand that perspective.

"As a woman, I know what you go through as a racial minority." This diminishes the uniqueness of the experience of the African American. While there may be similarities, a white woman's experience is not the same as an African American's. It would be like saying, "I had breast cancer and you had colon cancer, so I understand your experience." They may have similarities, but they are different.

"We are looking to hire more minorities, as long as they are qualified." Putting the caveat of "qualified" with "minorities" suggests that the speaker believes minorities are less qualified.

Angry Black Woman or Angry Black Man. There is a stereotype that black people are an angry lot, especially black women, though black men are often depicted this way as well. A few years ago I offered my opinion on some aspect of diversity at a conference. Later, I heard that someone there wanted to meet me, or specifically, he wanted to meet the person who was "ranting." I was really taken aback. I knew I was passionate, but *ranting?* No way. I interpreted that as a very negative description. African American directness and expressiveness are often confused as anger.

For **American Indians**, the following terms and popular idioms may be considered offensive:[1]

"Hey, Chief." If the American Indian addressed this way is not in fact a chief, this is considered insulting.

Squaw. This is considered a very derogatory term, referring to a woman's sexual organs.

"Hold down the fort." Historically, forts in America were built to hold back the Indians. To an American Indian, this implies that Indians are always on the "war path."

Pow-wow. In American Indian tradition, a pow-wow is a social gathering for ceremonial purposes. To refer to a quick meeting as a pow-wow trivializes that custom and could be offensive.

Low man on the totem pole. While this idiom might not be offensive, it could be considered insensitive. There is actually no hierarchy of importance connected with the images carved on totem poles.

Indian giver. This means that you give something away and then take it back. It is considered derogatory to American Indians. It may refer to the attempts by early settlers to buy land from American Indians, who at the time had no concept of land ownership and therefore did not understand that they were signing over their land.

Redskin. There has been a great deal of controversy and polarization about the use of this term as the name of Washington, DC's football team. It is considered offensive and disrespectful because the term was used throughout history in a pejorative way to describe American Indians. It is a derogatory slur that is akin to calling a black person the "N" word.

Here are comments and questions to avoid and attitudes to watch out for when interacting with **Asian American** employees:[2]

"Where are you from?" When the answer is the United States, the secondary question is usually, "No, really, where are you from originally?" The answer may still likely be the United States. This question is offensive because it can be interpreted as "You don't belong here" or "You are not as American as I am."

"You speak good English." The implication here is that most Asians do not speak "good" English.

"Can you recommend a good Chinese/Thai/Vietnamese/ sushi restaurant?" Just because a person is of Asian descent does not mean he or she is an expert on good Asian restaurants.

Claims that Asians are not discriminated against because they are prevalent in professional occupations, such as doctors and IT professionals.

Assuming that Asian kids excel in schools. This stereotype is offensive because it is limiting and makes sweeping generalizations about a group.

"You don't act very Asian." Again, this is a very stereotypical comment. What is an Asian supposed to act like? Treat people as individuals, not as a group stereotype.

"You all look alike." This may be the perception of someone who has had limited exposure to different Asian cultures, but it is another way of lumping everyone from one group, which ignores their individuality. (As mentioned in Chapter 3, gaining more exposure and experience helps one learn to differentiate.)

"Asians are not good leaders." There is a widespread assumption that Asians are not interested in leadership roles. Asian employees who do not have Western roots might have a different, quieter leadership style that is not as valued in Western culture. (People with this mindset might consider expanding their interpretation of desired leadership qualities.)

"Why are you so quiet? You need to speak up more." This kind of mandate suggests the person requiring this behavior is not very culturally competent and isn't aware that there is more than one way to engage and that cultural behaviors vary. Rather than dictating new behaviors that fit in one's own cultural framework, it would be better to incorporate different methods of obtaining input.

Model minority. This designation, given to Asians because a large majority are seen as successful and highly educated, is still a gross generalization and therefore overlooks the issues of inequality that are uniquely faced by Asian Americans. Model Minority Mutiny is an attempt for the Asian American community to dispel the model minority myth.

The term **Oriental**. While it is not universally considered offensive, in the United States it is at the very least outdated. President Obama signed an order to eliminate the use of the term in all federal documents. Some opponents of the term believe it reinforces the perpetual foreigner stereotype often associated with Asian Americans, thus justifying exclusion of and discrimination against Asian Americans.[3] (Note: In Britain, the word *Oriental* is still used as a generic term to describe Chinese or Southeast Asian people, mostly because the word *Asian* in the UK is used to describe people from India, Pakistan, and Bangladesh.)

Asia is very big continent comprised of numerous cultures. It is not useful to make sweeping generalities about Asians, or any group, for that matter. Learn to distinguish different cultural groups.

Gender inequality is a serious concern around the globe. While women make up half of the world's population, they continue to face serious inequities from a socio-economic perspective. In many organizations, women's upward mobility still lags; thus, the **glass ceiling** continues to persist.

As pointed out in Chapter 1, men are half as likely as women to believe that women are still held back from reaching their full potential, even though research supports that equally qualified women are less likely to be promoted. According to a study by LeanIn.Org and McKinsey & Co., women and men have equal aspirations for promotions; however, women are 15 percent less likely to make it to the next level in the organization.[4]

Here is a sampling of triggering comments and micro-inequities related to **gender**:

"Women are too emotional to be good leaders." Women may have learned to be more relationship oriented, to be nice, and to get along with others, while boys may have learned to compete, to be brave, and not to cry. Men may have been socialized to believe they are supposed to protect women and not take direction from them. Contemporary research suggests that good leaders have a blend of qualities that include emotional intelligence—being in touch with their own emotions and the emotions of others—making them more able to empathize and lead from the heart.

"Are you planning on having a family?" This is actually an illegal question in the United States. However, I have heard that it is still asked.

"Work-life balance is a woman's issue." Work-life balance is a *human* issue. Both men and women must balance their work and personal responsibilities.

"Women are not as good in math or technical roles." This is a persistent stereotype that is just not true. Men do not have more natural abilities in math and science. Studies show that the differential is due to social conditioning and the perpetuation of the stereotype.

"Women are not as committed to their careers." Gallup research suggests that women are actually more engaged than men in the workplace.[5]

When a woman speaks, her voice is often not heard. A man can offer the same input and he is more likely to be recognized for the contribution. During President Obama's administration, high-ranking women were intentional about fixing this problem. They called it "amplification." They would repeat an idea of a female colleague and give her credit for the idea by name. The impact was that more women were being seen as valuable members of the team.[6]

Women are more likely to be judged by outward appearances than their contributions. Research shows that "attractive" people—both men and women—earn higher salaries. Women, however, are held to an even higher standard. Throughout her political career, Hillary Clinton was often criticized for her dress and facial expressions. During a trip to Bangladesh in 2014, the headlines focused on the fact that she decided to give a speech at Dhaka International School without makeup, rather than on the purpose of her talk.[7]

Some triggering comments and questions for **Latino** workers include the following:

"You don't look like a Latino." We may have a preconceived notion of what someone from Latin, Central, or South America should look like. Latinos come from all different racial and ethnic groups and many different countries, and therefore there is no such thing as a *Latino look.*

"Do you speak Spanish, or do you speak English?" The assumption that someone with a Latin heritage should speak Spanish is stereotypical, as is the assumption that the person may not speak English. Latinos may be second- or even third-generation Americans and may not speak Spanish. A Latino may be bilingual, speak only English, or speak only Spanish.

"Your English is so good." Why would you expect it not to be?

"Can you recommend a good landscaper or housekeeper?" The assumption is that most Latinos do landscaping or housekeeping work and therefore any Latino must know someone who does.

"I know a number of Mexican people." Not all Latinos are Mexican. What message is the speaker trying to convey by saying this? That he or she understands the person being addressed? That he or she is not prejudiced? Claiming to know Mexican people is probably irrelevant to the conversation.

"Tone it down. Why are you so emotional?" For some Latino cultures, animated discourse is a sign of enthusiasm and passion. For some Euro-American cultures, strong emotional expressiveness is seen as a distraction and inappropriate. (See Chapter 3.) Being told to tone it down can actually result in someone "shutting down."

"Do you speak Mexican?" Mexico is a country, not a language. Spanish is the official language of Mexico.

Illegal immigrant. As pointed out in Chapter 3, this term is offensive. It is labeling the person and not the action. It is judgmental language. There is still a presumption of innocence until a jury has convicted an individual.

Examples of comments that can be insensitive to the **LGBTQ community** include the following:[8]

"I never would have guessed you were gay." While perhaps well intended, this comment has a judgmental tone. It could be interpreted as "I thought you were 'normal' like me."

"I suspected you were gay." This type of comment plays into stereotypes and can come across with a judgmental tone.

(To a transgender person) "What did you look like before?" It is inappropriate to talk about the past with a transgender person. Their current gender identity is who they are and should be affirmed.

"I have a gay friend that you should meet." No one should assume that a coworker would automatically want to meet that person's gay friend. Not all gay people are friends, just as not all straight people are friends.

"Your lifestyle is your business. We should not talk about that at work." Sexual orientation is not a choice the way a lifestyle is. The ability to bring one's whole self to work enhances engagement. Being able to include one's partner in office small talk or bringing the partner to work functions is part of being in an inclusive environment.

"I'm sorry." When spoken as a response to a coworker who has shared a part of their identity with you, this statement is judgmental. Why would you be sorry for that?

"What do gay people think about _____?" One gay person does not speak for the entire gay community. This is true for any of the groups discussed here. It is inappropriate to ask one person of a certain identity to speak for everyone in that group. Treat people as individuals.

In Chapter 1, I mentioned that conversations around disability and individuals with disabilities are not necessarily polarizing. However, this topic is one that we shy away from discussing, mostly due to our fear of offending. People with disabilities have struggled to move beyond being depicted as one-dimensional sources of inspiration who offer others an opportunity to be heroically inclusive. They are more likely to be invisible and under-recognized for their capabilities and contributions. The stigma surrounding disability leads many people and their allies to be reluctant to self-identify, even if they need an accommodation. Here are some micro-inequities, and triggering words and phrases for **people with disabilities**:[9]

"What is wrong with you?" While this may be a well-meaning question in an effort to be supportive, it is offensive. The term *wrong* is negative and the opposite is *right*, so it connotes that the person is not legitimate. It is especially inappropriate if one does not know the person well and has not built a trusting relationship. Some people with disabilities would prefer not to talk about their conditions. In order to engage in an inclusive conversation, it would be better to ask if the person would like to talk about his or her disability. If the answer is yes, the person with the disability should be allowed to describe the condition, and the person who asked should just listen. (See Chapter 5.)

"Were you born that way?" The person with a disability may wonder, was I born *what* way? This can be an intrusive

question, depending on the relationship. Again, it has a negative connotation.

"I don't think of you as a person with a disability." This is like saying I don't see you as a black person or an Asian. I realize that often when someone says this, the intent is assurance of equality. ("I don't see you as any different from me.") It is often heard by the person with a disability, however, as "Then you don't really see me. I *am* different, and that is okay."

Speaking more slowly or loudly to a person in a wheelchair. Our unconscious biases may lead us to assume that a person in a wheelchair also has other limitations and it might be an automatic response to speak louder or more slowly. Catch yourself if you do this. It is a part of the introspection and reflection process that I have discussed throughout the book.

Assuming that a person with a visible disability wants your help. As inclusion allies, we want to be helpful. Don't assume; ask the person if and how you can be helpful.

"How do you go to the bathroom?" This is also a very intrusive question. Even if someone is trying to learn more about the other person, as is advised in Chapter 3, this would probably not be a good question to pursue. It is private and personal and may make the other person feel very uncomfortable.

"You really look good." The implication is that this is a surprise because a person with disabilities would *not* look good. Again, this is probably a well-intended statement that is meant to be supportive, especially if someone has been out of work for a while with an illness. However, it can come across as "You look good for someone *in your condition*." Or, the person might hear it as "I really didn't

have high expectations about how you would look." It might be better to say, "Good to have you back. Let me know if and how I can support you."

There are also sentiments that historically marginalized groups should avoid saying to **white people**, including the following:

"You could never understand my issues." While I have contended throughout the book that it is really hard to walk in another's shoes, there are many white people who do understand, want to understand, and want to be allies.

"All white people are racist." We are all *biased*, but I don't believe that all white people are racist—that they consciously believe that black people and other historically marginalized groups are inferior and purposefully discriminate (take action) based on that belief.

"You are just a typical white person." What is a typical white person? This is a very stereotypical comment—a narrow, limited perspective on an entire group of people. People are individuals.

"You are not diverse." Everyone is diverse. We are each unique. Diversity is more than race. It includes age, gender, gender identity, background, religion, sexual orientation, and so on. No two people are exactly alike. Two white men may be different in many ways—age, occupation, religion, geographic location, interests, and so on. All of the aforementioned dimensions of diversity influence who we are.

"All white people are privileged." Privilege is relative. (See the discussion of privilege in Chapter 2.) We all have some level of privilege in various contexts. For example, there are black people who have socio-economic privilege over white people. To cast an entire group as

privileged without knowing individual circumstances fuels polarization. While white privilege exists, it is conferred and not asked for in many cases. Playing the white privilege card makes many white people feel guilty, which stymies inclusive conversations. It does not help to state the obvious.

Religion is a very difficult topic for the workplace. In general, like politics, ad hoc discussions about religion should probably be avoided. Structured conversations as I have described in the book can be useful in helping people to learn about each other's religions. A handful of major companies (e.g., Ford, Aetna, and American Express) have started faith-based employee resource groups.[10]

For example, Ford's Interfaith Network (FIN), is one of eleven company-approved employee groups. Its board members represent eight faiths—Buddhism, Catholicism, Judaism, Evangelical Christian, Islam, Hinduism, Orthodox Christianity, and the Church of Jesus Christ of Latter-day Saints; however, all are welcome to join. There are also "Other Affiliates," including Asatru, Baha'i faith, Humanism, Sikhism, Jainism, Spiritism, Paganism, Unitarianism, Zoroastrianism, and Universalism.

The primary purpose of faith-based employee resource groups is to educate employees about religious diversity. Companies believe that such networks can also help with recruitment and increase employee engagement.

The coordinated efforts to educate about different **religious beliefs** is a positive step. However, we still have to be mindful of discussions that are off-limits. The following should not be allowed in workplaces:

Proselytizing. It is totally inappropriate for employees to try to convert others to their religion.

Denigrating someone else's religion. While you may totally disagree with someone else's beliefs, you should respect that they have the right to them.

Offering prayer or some other spiritual practice to someone who is not interested. We have to know when to keep our religious beliefs to ourselves and not force them on to others.

In general, for any group, if you want to increase the likelihood of having an effective bold, inclusive conversation, you should avoid these types of phrases:

"I think you are being overly sensitive." How would you know? If you have not had the experience, you cannot judge the other person's response. This is demeaning and dismissive. It is better to ask, "Why is this important to you?"

"That's not anything to worry about." Perhaps it is not anything for you to worry about, but you cannot know what the other person's reason for worrying might be.

"I know how you feel." You really don't know how someone else feels. It is better to say, "Help me to understand how that makes you feel."

"Calm down." This can be triggering for someone who doesn't feel that they are being overly emotional. It might be better to say, "I see that you have a lot of passion around this topic." However if the person is visibly angry, it might be best to say, "Let's talk about this tomorrow after we have both had an opportunity to think about it more."

"I have a lot of friends who are _____" (fill in any group). This is offensive because it implies that just because you have friends from the same racial, ethnic, or religious group as the person you're addressing that you could not be biased. Or if you are saying something else, what are you trying to convey?

FINAL THOUGHTS: PUT YOUR HEART IN
IT AND COMMIT TO LIVE INCLUSIVELY

We will never have all the right answers of what to say or what to do when we are attempting bold, inclusive conversations. There is usually more than one right answer, which is why this work is hard.

This is a guide; the work is a *journey*. Don't try to memorize all the dos and don'ts. There are too many of them, and they will keep changing anyway. If your heart is in the right place and you genuinely have a desire to learn how to have the tough conversations on the topics that seem to continue to polarize our society, you will be fine. You will make mistakes along the way because learning by its very definition is about making mistakes. Hopefully we will all learn the skill of patience to allow more of us to grow together in our quest to make this a more inclusive world.

I invite you to commit to Live Inclusively by signing the pledge below and inviting others to do the same!

Commitment to Live Inclusively

- I commit to be intentional in living inclusively.

- I commit to spending more time getting to know myself and understanding my culture. It is in understanding myself that I am better positioned to understand others. I will acknowledge that I don't know what I don't know, but I will not use what is unconscious as an excuse.

- I will be intentional in exposing myself to difference. If I don't know, I will ask. If I am asked, I will assume positive intent. Most importantly, I will accept my responsibility in increasing my own knowledge and understanding.

- I commit to speaking up and speaking out, even when I am not directly impacted, for there is no such thing as neutrality in the quest for equity, justice, and inclusion.

- I will strive to accept, and not just tolerate; respect, even if I don't agree; and be curious, not judgmental. I commit to pausing and listening. I will be empathetic to the experiences and perspectives of my "others." I will use my privilege positively and get comfortable with my own discomfort.

- I commit to knowing, getting, and doing better than I did yesterday—keeping in mind that my commitment to live inclusively is a journey, not a destination.

Your signature

CHAPTER 7 ◆ TIPS FOR TALKING ABOUT IT!

- Polarizing topics will not always be front and center in the workplace, but it is important to be ready for the conversations when they arise.

- There are inclusive habits that you should hone and practice on a regular basis.

- Avoid words and phrases that may be offensive, insensitive, or outdated as you learn to converse with different groups.

- Don't try to memorize a list of dos and don'ts because they are a moving target and there is always more than one right answer.

- Come from your heart, learn from your mistakes, and commit to continuing to contribute to making this a more inclusive world for all.

- Take the pledge to Live Inclusively.

- Invite other to take the pledge to Live Inclusively!

Glossary

Acceptance: An ethnorelative mindset on the Intercultural Development Continuum where individuals recognize and appreciate patterns of cultural difference and commonality in their own and other cultures.

Accommodation Style: An intercultural conflict style preferred by many Asian cultures and characterized as indirect and emotionally restrained.

Adaptation: An ethnorelative orientation on the Intercultural Development Continuum that is capable of shifting cultural perspective and changing behavior in culturally appropriate and authentic ways. Adaptation involves both deep cultural bridging across diverse communities and an increased repertoire of cultural frameworks and practices available to draw upon in reconciling cultural commonalities and differences.

Civil Rights Act of 1964: The landmark civil rights and labor law in the United States that outlaws discrimination based on race, color, religion, sex, or national origin.

Cultural Humility: The ability to maintain an interpersonal stance that is other-oriented (or open to the other) in relation to aspects of cultural identity that are most important to the person.

Cultural Identity: Feeling or sense of belonging to a specific social group (nationality, ethnicity, religion, class, generation, etc.) that has its own distinct culture. Cultural identity can be characteristic of the individual or shared characteristics among group members.

Culture: Shared beliefs, social norms, and traits of a social group. A set of shared attitudes, values, goals, and practices that characterize an organization.

Denial: A mindset on the Intercultural Development Continuum that reflects less capability for understanding and appropriately responding to cultural differences. Individuals with a denial orientation often do not recognize differences in perceptions and behavior as cultural. A denial orientation is characteristic of individuals who have limited experience with other cultural groups and therefore tend to operate with broad stereotypes and generalizations about the cultural other.

Disability: A condition or function that results in challenges associated with performing daily life activities such as walking, seeing, hearing.

Discussion Style: An intercultural conflict style characterized as direct and emotionally restrained. This style is most preferred by Euro-American, Northern European, and Canadian cultures.

Dominant Group: A group with systemic power, privileges, and social status within a society. Dominant does not imply *majority*. In the US context, dominant groups include white, male, heterosexual identities.

Dynamic Style: An intercultural conflict style common among Middle Eastern cultures, characterized as indirect and emotionally expressive.

Education: (One of the 4Es) Gaining new knowledge and skills through instruction, study, and experiences.

Empathy: (One of the 4Es) Experience of understanding another person's condition from their perspective. You place yourself in their shoes and feel what they are feeling.

Engagement Style: An intercultural conflict style characterized as direct and emotionally expressive, most commonly found among African Americans, Greeks, some Western Europeans, and Latino cultures.

Ethnocentric Worldview: Mindsets/orientations that assume the worldview of one's own culture is central to reality. (See also Denial and Polarization.)

Ethnorelative: A mindset that supposes cultures can only be understood relative to one another, and that particular behaviors can only be understood within a cultural context. (See also Acceptance and Adaptation.)

Experience: (One of the 4Es) The extent to which one has intimately encountered, engaged with, and gained knowledge from being exposed to difference.

Exposure: (One of the 4Es) The extent to which one comes in contact with cultural differences and diversity.

Glass Ceiling: A metaphor used to represent an invisible barrier that keeps a given demographic (typically applied to women) from rising beyond a certain level in a hierarchy.

Historically Marginalized Groups: Societal groups that have been traditionally oppressed, excluded, or disadvantaged.

Intercultural Conflict Style Inventory: A cross-culturally validated assessment of an individual's approach to communicating, resolving conflicts, and solving problems.

Intercultural Development Continuum: A theoretical framework that ranges from the more monocultural mindsets of Denial and Polarization through the transitional orientation of Minimization to the intercultural or global mindsets of Acceptance and Adaptation.

Intersectionality: A term coined by scholar Kimberlé Crenshaw that describes the study of intersecting social identities (race, gender, class, etc.) and related systems of oppression. Intersectionality theory posits that multiple identities/isms are not mutually exclusive; rather, they intersect to create unique experiences.

Ladder of Inference: Describes the thinking process that we go through, usually without realizing it, to get from a fact to a decision or action. The thinking stages can be seen as rungs on a ladder.

LGBTQ: An abbreviation that originated in the 1990s and replaced what was formerly known as the gay community. The abbreviation was created to be more inclusive of diverse groups. LGBTQ stands for lesbian, gay, bisexual, transgender, and queer (and/or questioning) individuals/identities.

Micro-inequities: Subtle, often unconscious, messages that single out, overlook, ignore, or otherwise discount individuals or groups based on aspects of their social identities (e.g., race, gender).

Minimization: A transitional mindset on the Intercultural Development Continuum that highlights cultural commonality and universal values and principles that can mask a deeper understanding and consideration of cultural differences. Minimization can take one of two forms: (a) the highlighting of similarities due to limited cultural self-awareness, which is more commonly experienced by dominant group members within a cultural community; or (b) the highlighting of similarities more deliberatively as a strategy for navigating the values and practices largely determined by the dominant culture group, which is more commonly experienced by nondominant group members within a larger cultural community.

Oriental: A somewhat outdated U.S. term used to describe people from East Asia. Now considered offensive by many when referencing people rather than objects.

Platinum Rule: An alternative to the widely known Golden Rule. The Platinum Rule encourages one to "Do unto others as they'd like done unto them."

Polarization: An orientation on the Intercultural Development Continuum that reflects a judgmental mindset that views cultural differences from an "us-versus-them" perspective. Polarization can take the form of defense ("My cultural practices are superior to other cultural practices") or reversal ("Other cultures are better than mine"). Within defense, cultural differences are often perceived as divisive and threatening to one's own cultural way of doing things, while reversal is a mindset that values and may idealize other cultural practices while denigrating those of one's own culture group. Reversal may also support the cause of an oppressed group, but this is done with little knowledge of what the cause means to people from the oppressed community.

Privilege: A social theory that posits special rights or advantages are available only to a particular person or group of people. The term is commonly used in the context of social inequality, particularly in regards to age, disability, ethnic or racial category, gender, sexual orientation, religion, and/or social class.

Reciprocal Learning: An instructional model where the traditional roles of mentor/coach and student/mentee are shared between the pair.

Reverse Mentoring: A process in which an individual in a dominant group learns from someone in a non-dominant group (e.g., a white male learns from an African American, or a baby boomer learns from a millennial).

Unconscious Bias: An unconscious judgment that happens automatically and is triggered by our brain making quick assessments of people and situations, influenced by our background, cultural environment, and personal experiences.

Notes

One

1. George Kohlrieser, "Leading at the edge," *Orchestrating Winning Performance* (2008): 193–197, http://www.georgekohlrieser.com/user files/file/articles/1.GK_LeadingAtTheEdge.pdf.

2. Race Forward Center for Racial Justice Innovation, "Race Reporting Guide: A Race Forward Media Reference," *Race Forward* (2015), New York, https://www.raceforward.org/sites/default/files/Race%20 Reporting%20Guide%20by%20Race%20Forward_V1.1.pdf (Date Accessed: 1/25/2017).

3. Radio One, Inc., "Black, White & Blue: A Spotlight on Race in America" (2016), Silver Spring, http://blackwhiteblue.newsone.com/ (Date Accessed: 1/25/2017).

4. The Winters Group, Inc., "Race & Workplace Trauma During the Age of #BlackLivesMatter" (2016), http://www.wintersgroup.com/ whitepapers-and-reports/.

5. Lisa McKenzie, "Brexit is the only way the working class can change anything," *Guardian* (2016), https://www.theguardian.com/ commentisfree/2016/jun/15/brexit-working-class-sick-racist-eu -referendum.

6. Zack Beauchamp, "Brexit, explained in one chart," *Vox* (2016), http://www.vox.com/2016/6/23/12012962/brexit-eu-referendum -time-polls-close-chart (Date accessed: 1/31/2017).

7. Robert P. Jones, Daniel Cox, Betsy Cooper, and Rachel Lienesch, "Anxiety, Nostalgia, and Mistrust: Findings from the 2015 American Values Survey," *PRRI* (2015), http://www.prri.org/research/survey

-anxiety-nostalgia-and-mistrust-findings-from-the-2015-american
-values-survey/ (Date Accessed: 1/31/2017).

8. Hannah Fingerhut, "In both parties, men and women differ over
whether women still face obstacles to progress," *PewResearchCenter*
(2016), http://www.pewresearch.org/fact-tank/2016/08/16/in-both
-parties-men-and-women-differ-over-whether-women-still-face
-obstacles-to-progress/ (Date Accessed: 1/31/2017).

9. Unilever, "Unilever urges world leaders to unstereotype the workplace," *Unilever News* (2017), https://www.unilever.com/news/news
-and-features/2017/Unilever-urges-world-leaders-to-unstereotype-the
-workplace.html (Date Accessed: 1/31/2017).

10. Pew Research Center, "A Wider Ideological Gap between More
and Less Educated Adults," *Pew Research Center U.S. Politics & Policy*
(2016), http://www.people-press.org/2016/04/26/a-wider-ideolog
ical-gap-between-more-and-less-educated-adults/ (Date Accessed:
1/31/2017).

11. Perry Stein, Steve Hendrix, and Abigail Hauslohner, "Women's
marches: More than one million protesters vow to resist President
Trump," *Washington Post* (2017), https://www.washingtonpost.com/
local/womens-march-on-washington-a-sea-of-pink-hatted-protesters
-vow-to-resist-donald-trump/2017/01/21/ae4def62-dfdf-11e6-acdf
-14da832ae861_story.html?utm_term=.7c56797d7399 (Date Accessed:
1/31/2017).

12. Rick Glazier, "18 Questions, 18 Answers: The Real Facts behind
House Bill 2," *North Carolina Justice Center* (2016), http://www.ncjustice
.org/?q=18-questions-18-answers-real-facts-behind-house-bill-2 (Date
Accessed: 1/31/2017).

13. Tate Walker, "3 Things You Need to Know about Indigenous
Efforts against the Dakota Access Pipeline," *Everyday Feminism* (2016),
http://everydayfeminism.com/2016/09/dakota-access-pipeline/ (Date
Accessed: 1/31/2017).

14. Jesse A. Steinfeldt, Lisa Rey Thomas, and Mattie R. White, "Legis-
lative efforts to eliminate native-themed mascots, nicknames, and logos:
Slow but steady progress post-APA resolution," *American Psychological
Association* (2010), http://www.apa.org/pi/oema/resources/communi
que/2010/08/native-themed-mascots.aspx (Date Accessed: 1/27/2017).

15. Brian Montopoli, "DREAM Act Dies in the Senate," *CBS* (2010),
http://www.cbsnews.com/news/dream-act-dies-in-the-senate-18-12
-2010/ (Date Accessed: 1/31/2017).

16. Hardeep Aiden and Andrea McCarthy, "Current attitudes towards
disabled people," *Scope about disability* (2014), http://www.scope.org

.uk/Scope/media/Images/Publication%20Directory/Current-attitudes
-towards-disabled-people.pdf (Date Accessed: 1/25/2017).

17. Author's interview of Kate Vernon (January 2017).

18. Gallup, Inc., "State of the American Workplace: Employee
Engagement Insights for U.S. Business Leaders," *GALLUP* (2013).

19. Jeanine Prime and Elizabeth R. Salib, "The Secret to Inclusion in
Australian Workplaces: Psychological Safety," Catalyst website (August
25, 2015).

20. Jessica McBride, "Philando Castile: 5 Fast Facts You Need to Know,"
Heavy (2016), http://heavy.com/news/2016/07/philando-castile
-falcon-heights-minnesota-police-shooting-facebook-live-video-watch
-uncensored-you-tube-police-shooting-man-shot-lavish-reynolds/ (Date
Accessed: 1/27/2017).

21. Ariel Zambelich, "3 Hours in Orlando: Piecing Together an Attack
and Its Aftermath," *NPR* (2016), http://www.npr.org/2016/06/16/
482322488/orlando-shooting-what-happened-update (Date Accessed:
1/31/2017).

22. Shawn Shinneman, "'Tolerance is for cowards' . . . AT&T CEO
Randall Stephenson speaks on racial tension and Black Lives Matter,"
BizJournals (2016), http://www.bizjournals.com/dallas/blog/techflash/
2016/10/tolerance-is-for-cowards-at-t-ceo-randall.html (Date Accessed:
1/31/2017).

Two

1. Catalyzing Change, "10 Lao Tzu Quotes for Healthy Thinking,"
Catalyzing Change (2014), http://www.catalyzingchange.org/10-lao-tzu
-quotes-for-healthy-living/ (Date Accessed: 1//31/2017).

2. Erik Homburger Erikson, *Identity: Youth and Crisis* (London: Faber
& Faber, 1968).

3. Kimberlé Crenshaw, "Demarginalizing the intersection of race and
sex: A black feminist critique of antidiscrimination doctrine, feminist
theory and antiracist politics," *U. Chi. Legal F.* (1989): 139.

4. Claude M. Steele, "A threat in the air: How stereotypes shape intellectual identity and performance," *American psychologist* 52, no. 6 (1997):
613.

5. Steven J. Spencer, Claude M. Steele, and Diane M. Quinn, "Stereotype threat and women's math performance," *Journal of experimental
social psychology* 35, no. 1 (1999): 4–28.

6. Claude M. Steele and Joshua Aronson, "Stereotype threat and the
intellectual test performance of African Americans," *Journal of personality
and social psychology* 69, no. 5 (1995): 797.

7. Caryn J. Block, Sandy M. Koch, Benjamin E. Liberman, Tarani J. Merriweather, and Loriann Roberson, "Contending with stereotype threat at work: A model of long-term responses 1–7," *The Counseling Psychologist* 39, no. 4 (2011): 570–600.

8. Marianne Williamson, *A Return to Love* (New York: HarperCollins Press, 2009).

9. Melanie Greenberg Ph.D., "The Six Attributes of Courage," *Psychology Today* (2012), https://www.psychologytoday.com/blog/the-mindful-self-express/201208/the-six-attributes-courage (Date Accessed: 1/31/2017).

10. Melanie Tervalon and Jann Murray-Garcia, "Cultural humility versus cultural competence: A critical distinction in defining physician training outcomes in multicultural education," *Journal of Health Care for the Poor and Underserved* (May 1998), 9, 2; ProQuest Medical Library p. 117.

11. Chimamanda Ngozi Adichie, "The danger of a single story," *TED-Global* (2009), https://www.ted.com/talks/chimamanda_adichie_the_danger_of_a_single_story?language=en (Date Accessed: 1/25/2017).

12. Kyoung-Ah Nam and John Condon, "The DIE is cast: The continuing evolution of intercultural communication's favorite classroom exercise," *International Journal of Intercultural Relations* (2010), 81–87.

13. Michael F. Broom, *Power: The Infinite Game* (Pelham, MA: HRD Press, 1995).

Three

1. Mellody Hobson, "Color blind or color brave?" *TED* (2014), https://www.ted.com/talks/mellody_hobson_color_blind_or_color_brave (Date Accessed: 1/27/2017).

2. Robert P. Jones, Daniel Cox, and Juhem Navarro-Rivera, "Race, Religion, and Political Affiliation of Americans' Core Social Networks," *PRRI* (2016), http://www.prri.org/research/poll-race-religion-politics-americans-social-networks/ (Date Accessed: 1/31/2017).

3. Robert P. Jones, Daniel Cox, Betsy Cooper, and Rachel Lienesch, "Anxiety, Nostalgia, and Mistrust: Findings from the 2015 American Values Survey," *PRRI* (2015), http://www.prri.org/research/survey-anxiety-nostalgia-and-mistrust-findings-from-the-2015-american-values-survey/ (Date Accessed: 1/31/2017).

4. Nicholas Carlson, "Meet Mitt Romney's Hero: His Surprisingly Liberal Dad," *Business Insider* (2012), http://www.businessinsider.com/mitt-romneys-father-george-romney-was-a-liberal-2012-8 (Date Accessed: 1/31/2017).

5. Gallup, Inc., "State of the American Workplace: Employee Engagement Insights for U.S. Business Leaders," GALLUP (2013).

6. Sylvia Ann Hewlett, Maggie Jackson, and Ellis Cose, "Vaulting the Color Bar: How sponsorship levers multicultural professionals into leaders," Center for Talent Innovation (2012).

7. Junot Diaz, *The Brief Wondrous Life of Oscar Wao* (New York: Riverhead Books, 2007).

8. Race Forward Center for Racial Justice Innovation, "Race Reporting Guide: A Race Forward Media Reference" (2015).

9. Ibid.

10. David Folkenflik, "NPR Ends Williams' Contract after Muslim Remarks," NPR (2010), http://www.npr.org/templates/story/story .php?storyId=130712737 (Date Accessed: 1/31/2017).

11. Sylvia Ann Hewlett, Melinda Marshall, and Laura Sherbin, "Innovation, Diversity, and Market Growth," Center for Talent Innovation (2013).

12. Paul J. Zak, "The Neuroscience of Trust," *Harvard Business Review*, January–February (2017).

13. Stephen R. Covey, *The SPEED of Trust: The One Thing That Changes Everything* (New York: Simon and Schuster, 2006).

14. Thomas Kochman, *Black and White Styles in Conflict* (Chicago: University of Chicago Press, 1981).

15. "Maya Angelou," *BrainyQuote.com*, Xplore Inc. (2017), https:// www.brainyquote.com/quotes/quotes/m/mayaangelo125778.html (Date Accessed 1/31/2017).

Five

1. "Criminal Justice Fact Sheet," NAACP (2017), http://www.naacp .org/criminal-justice-fact-sheet/ (Date Accessed: 1/31/2017).

2. Edwin S. Rubenstein, "The Color of Crime: Race, Crime, and Justice in America," New Century Foundation (2016).

3. Ann E. Carson, Ph.D., "Prisoners in 2013," *U.S. Department of Justice Office of Justice Programs Bulletin* (September 2014).

4. Howard Zinn, Kathy Emery, and Ellen Reeves, *The People's History of the United States: A New Press People's History Series* (New York: The New Press, 1980).

5. Nell Irvin Painter, *The History of White People* (New York: W.W. Norton & Company, 2011).

6. Mark Peffley and Jon Hurwitz, *Justice in America: The Separate Realities of Blacks and Whites* (Cambridge: Cambridge University Press, 2010).

7. Michelle Alexander, *The New Jim Crow: Mass Incarceration in the Age of Colorblindness* (New York: The New Press, 2012).

8. Ava DuVernay, *13th: From Slave to Criminal with One Amendment,* Netflix, October, 2016.

9. Peter M. Senge, *The Fifth Discipline Fieldbook: Strategies and Tools for Building a Learning Organization* (New York: Currency Double Day, 1994).

10. GoodReads, "John Dewey," *Quotable Quote,* http://www.good reads.com/quotes/664197-we-do-not-learn-from-experience-we-learn -from-reflecting (Date Accessed: 1/27/2017).

Six

1. Maya Angelou, *I Know Why the Caged Bird Sings* (New York: Random House, 1996).

2. Pew Research Center, "On Views of Race and Inequality, Blacks and Whites Are Worlds Apart," June 27, 2016.

3. ThinkExist, "Chris Cavanaugh Quotes," http://thinkexist.com/ quotation/storytellers-by_the_very_act_of_telling/171808.html (Date Accessed: 1/27/2017).

Seven

1. DiversityInc, "Things NOT to Say to American Indian Coworkers" (2013), http://www.diversityinc.com/things-not-to-say/things-never -to-say-to-american-indian-coworkers/ (Date Accessed: 1/31/2017).

2. Stacy Straczynski, "7 Things NOT to Say to Asian-Americans," *DiversityInc* (2013) http://www.diversityinc.com/things-not-to-say/7 -things-not-to-say-to-asian-americans/ (Date Accessed: 1/31/2017).

3. Jayne Tsuchiyama, "The term 'Oriental' is outdated, but is it racist?" *Los Angeles Times* (2016), http://www.latimes.com/opinion/op-ed/ la-oe-tsuchiyama-oriental-insult-20160601-snap-story.html (Date Accessed: 1/31/2017).

4. McKinsey & Company, "Women in the Workplace 2016," LeanIn .org (2016).

5. Gallup, Inc., "State of the American Workplace: Employee Engagement Insights for U.S. Business Leaders," GALLUP (2013).

6. Keli Goff, "How the Women of the Obama White House Fought Gender Inequality—and We Can Too," *The Daily Beast* (2016), http:// www.thedailybeast.com/articles/2016/09/23/how-the-women-of-the -obama-white-house-fought-gender-inequality-and-we-can-too.html (Date Accessed: 1/25/2017).

7. Eve Tahmincioglu, "For women in the workplace, it's still about

looks not deeds," *TODAY* (2012), http://www.today.com/money/ women-workplace-its-still-about-looks-not-deeds-772762 (Date Accessed: 1/25/2017).

8. DiversityInc, "Things NOT to say to an LGBT CoWorker," DiversityInc (2013), http://www.diversityinc.com/diversity-and-inclusion/ slideshow-things-not-to-say-to-an-lgbt-coworker/ (Date Accessed: 1/25/2017).

9. DiversityInc, "7 Things Never to Say to People with Disabilities," DiversityInc (2008), http://www.diversityinc.com/things-not-to -say/7-things-never-to-say-to-people-with-disabilities/ (Date Accessed: 1/31/2017).

10. DiversityInc, "Starting Religious Employee Resource Groups," DiversityInc (2009), http://www.diversityinc.com/resource-groups-2/ starting-religious-employee-resource-groups/ (Date Accessed: 1/30/2017).

Acknowledgments

I acknowledge my amazing children, Joseph and Mareisha, my late husband, Joseph, and my dedicated partner, Ken.

I acknowledge The Winters Group team. A special thank you to Brittany Harris, who served as my internal editor, and Travis Jones, who was an early reader and adviser.

A BIG thanks to Julie O'Mara, a diversity and inclusion thought leader who pushed me to write the book and has offered invaluable advice.

I want to thank the Berrett-Koehler team, especially Steve Piersanti, who believed in my vision for this book and was there every step of the way with encouragement, wisdom, and unconditional support.

I acknowledge *all* of my many colleagues and friends in the diversity and inclusion field who have dedicated their lives to advancing inclusion. I have learned so much from them.

I acknowledge The Winters Group clients, with whom I have the honor of working on an ongoing basis in their efforts for inclusion.

Index

About the Author

MARY-FRANCES WINTERS came of age during the Civil Rights Movement of the 1960s. An advocate for equity since her days as editor of her high school newspaper, as CEO of The Winters Group for the past 33 years she has consulted with all different types of organizations in their quest for inclusion. Prior to founding The Winters Group, she was an affirmative action officer and senior market analyst at Eastman Kodak Company.

She has received many awards and distinctions, including the ATHENA Leadership Award (presented to a woman or man for professional excellence, community service, and for actively assisting women in their attainment of professional excellence and leadership skills); The Hutchinson Medal from her alma mater, The University of Rochester (given annually to an alum in recognition of outstanding achievement and notable service to the community, state, or nation); and The Winds of Change Award, conferred by the University of St. Thomas at the Forum on Workplace Inclusion, for her efforts to change lives, organizations, and communities. She was also recognized as a diversity pioneer by *Profiles in Diversity Journal*.

A life member of the Board of Trustees of the University of Rochester, Ms. Winters has served on the boards of the Chamber of Commerce, The United Way, and the National Board of the Girl Scouts of the USA. She also served as a mentor for the Emerging Leaders Program, sponsored by the Centers for Leadership and Public Values at Duke University and the University of Cape Town, South Africa.

Winters is the author of three other books: *Inclusion Starts with I, CEOs Who Get It: Diversity Leadership from the Heart and Soul,* and *Only Wet Babies Like Change: Workplace Wisdom for Baby Boomers.*

Described by clients as innovative, collaborative, visionary, and results-oriented, she is also a provocateur—provoking conversation and encouraging dialogue—and she is not afraid to have the tough conversations. Her sweet spots include helping organizations develop their diversity and inclusion strategy, developing culturally competent leaders, and serving as a mentor and coach.

ABOUT THE WINTERS GROUP

THE WINTERS GROUP, INC. is a minority- and women-owned diversity and inclusion and organizational development consulting firm headquartered outside of Washington, DC. For 33 years The Winters Group has inspired ingenuity through inclusion, by supporting organizations, large and small, to develop sustainable diversity and inclusion strategies for game-changing organizational performance.

The Winters Group's vision is a world that values, respects, and leverages our similarities and differences. Our mission is to create transformative and sustainable solutions for individuals and organizations in support of their efforts to create more equitable and inclusive environments. The Winters Group has helped hundreds of Fortune 100 companies, not-for-profit organizations, educational institutions, and the government succeed with organizational change by developing, executing, and measuring strategies that lead to breakthrough results. The Winters Group's core offerings have an emphasis in ethnic and multicultural issues:

Organization Development	Cultural Audits (surveys, focus groups, interviews)
Leadership Development	
Diversity and Inclusion Strategy Development	Executive Coaching
	Training and Education
Change Management	Keynote Speaking

Berrett–Koehler
Publishers

Berrett-Koehler is an independent publisher dedicated to an ambitious mission: *Connecting people and ideas to create a world that works for all.*

We believe that the solutions to the world's problems will come from all of us, working at all levels: in our organizations, in our society, and in our own lives. Our BK Business books help people make their organizations more humane, democratic, diverse, and effective (we don't think there's any contradiction there). Our BK Currents books offer pathways to creating a more just, equitable, and sustainable society. Our BK Life books help people create positive change in their lives and align their personal practices with their aspirations for a better world.

All of our books are designed to bring people seeking positive change together around the ideas that empower them to see and shape the world in a new way.

And we strive to practice what we preach. At the core of our approach is Stewardship, a deep sense of responsibility to administer the company for the benefit of all of our stakeholder groups including authors, customers, employees, investors, service providers, and the communities and environment around us. Everything we do is built around this and our other key values of quality, partnership, inclusion, and sustainability.

This is why we are both a B-Corporation and a California Benefit Corporation—a certification and a for-profit legal status that require us to adhere to the highest standards for corporate, social, and environmental performance.

We are grateful to our readers, authors, and other friends of the company who consider themselves to be part of the BK Community. We hope that you, too, will join us in our mission.

A BK Business Book

We hope you enjoy this BK Business book. BK Business books pioneer new leadership and management practices and socially responsible approaches to business. They are designed to provide you with groundbreaking and practical tools to transform your work and organizations while upholding the triple bottom line of people, planet, and profits. High-five!

To find out more, visit **www.bkconnection.com**.

Berrett–Koehler
Publishers

Connecting people and ideas
to create a world that works for all

Dear Reader,

Thank you for picking up this book and joining our worldwide community of Berrett-Koehler readers. We share ideas that bring positive change into people's lives, organizations, and society.

To welcome you, we'd like to offer you a free e-book. You can pick from among twelve of our bestselling books by entering the promotional code BKP92E here: http://www.bkconnection.com/welcome.

When you claim your free e-book, we'll also send you a copy of our e-newsletter, the *BK Communiqué*. Although you're free to unsubscribe, there are many benefits to sticking around. In every issue of our newsletter you'll find

- A free e-book
- Tips from famous authors
- Discounts on spotlight titles
- Hilarious insider publishing news
- A chance to win a prize for answering a riddle

Best of all, our readers tell us, "Your newsletter is the only one I actually read." So claim your gift today, and please stay in touch!

Sincerely,

Charlotte Ashlock
Steward of the BK Website

Questions? Comments? Contact me at bkcommunity@bkpub.com.

Certified

Corporation
bcorporation.net